Founded in 1983, Sunrise Medical Limited offer
an extensive selection of mobility products
from some of the industry's popular b

- Paediatric Manual Wheelchairs
- Standard Manual Wheelchairs
- Configurable Folding Manual Wheelchairs
- Configurable Rigid Manual Wheelchairs
- Folding Powered Wheelchairs
- Rigid Powered Wheelchairs
- Scooters

For further information on the Sunrise Medical family of products or to request your free brochure please contact Customer Services on

01384 44 66 22

QUICKIE
STERLING

INNOVATE.
BUILD FOR THE FUTURE

Mobility and General Information Centre

Call us free for motoring and mobility information

Lots of people are calling MAGIC - drivers of Motability Scheme vehicles, people who would like information on how to obtain one, carers, mature drivers and medical professionals working with people with mobility issues. They all share one need, to obtain information from one source.

Our staff provide reliable and practical information and can help with any query - from how to arrange a vehicle test drive and getting it adapted, to how to get in touch with help groups or companies specialising in accessible holidays. Twenty percent of our staff have experienced disabilities and everyone has been through a comprehensive training programme, so you'll always be talking to someone who understands. One free call is all it takes.

But don't just take our word for it, call MAGIC free on 0800 240 241

E-mail: help@fordmagic.co.uk
www.fordmagic.co.uk

London Blue Badge Parking Guide

www.thePIEguide.com

CONTENTS

Foreword	5
Editors notes	7
Useful Information	10-13
Key to map pages	14
London Boroughs map	15
Key to map symbols	16-17
Street mapping	18-49
Index to street names	50-75
Shopping centre maps:	
Croydon	76
Greenwich	77
Kingston	78
Shopmobility	79
Blue Badge parking concessions by Councils across London	80-81
Congestion Charge for Blue Badge Holders	82
Airport parking maps:	
Luton & City Airports	83
Heathrow Airport	84
Gatwick Airport	85
Stansted Airport	87
Useful contact numbers	90
Directory of Services	93-95
Have your say	96

Collins

Specially produced for PIE Enterprises Ltd by Collins, a subsidiary of HarperCollins*Publishers* Ltd.
Mapping © Collins Bartholomew 2004   Tel: 01242 258155

Information specific for the Blue Badge user supplied by PIE
Enterprises Ltd © 2004.   Tel: 0207 324 6276
All rights reserved www.thePIEguide.com

Disclaimer
Every possible effort has been taken to ensure that the information given in this publication is accurate whilst the publishers would be grateful to learn of any errors, users should be aware that this information may change at any time. Parking bays, lines and signs may be moved to accommodate new traffic schemes, resurfacing, road works or many other reasons, they regret they cannot accept any responsibility for loss thereby caused.

Special thanks to the help & support from:
Mike Hudson
Operations & Content Manager
Information Providers:
London Councils & TfL

PIE Enterprises Ltd and any of its sponsors take no responsibility whatsoever for where a car is parked for any consequences arising from parking at any location authorised or not. Published by PIE Enterprises Ltd, ©2004. All rights reserved. No reproduction by any method whatsoever of any part of this publication is permitted without prior written consent of the copyright owners.

General Enquires & Trade Sales
Telephone: 0870 444 5434, Fax: 0870 444 5437
email: enquires@thePIEguide.com

WWW.thePIEguide.com

ISBN 0-00-772609-0
Printed in Hong Kong

Publishers/Cartographers:
Collins Maps & Atlases, Robert & Jackie
Our team of surveyors:
Lisa, Simon D, Mario, Damien, Daiva & Simon L

Advertising Sales:
Emma Bosanquet
Layout & Design:
mabox

Keeping you moving
Breakdown cover for Blue Badge holders

Response is a comprehensive breakdown package offered exclusively to Blue Badge Holders.

Membership means we'll alert a patrol that you are a Response Member before they reach you. You can even call a patrol out to your home, if your car won't start.

In addition, in the unlikely event that we're unable to fix your car at the roadside within a reasonable time, we'll provide:

– a tow to any mainland UK destination

– provide overnight accommodation

– arrange for you to complete your journey by taxi, train or plane

For instant cover call now on
0800 0722 822

Phone lines are open: Mon to Fri 8am-9pm, Sat 9am-5pm, Sun 10am-4pm.

For Personal Finance, **Insurance**, BSM Lessons, **Injury Claims** and Windscreen Repairs **call 08000 966 000**

Full terms and conditions apply. Certain of the benefits and services are classed as general insurance, provided by RAC Motoring Services and/or RAC Insurance Ltd (Company Nos. 1424399 and 2355834). Registered office: RAC House, 1 Forest Road, Feltham, TW13 7RR. Members of the General Insurance Standards Council. Insurance policies are governed by the laws of England and Wales. RAC Insurance Limited is authorised and regulated by the Financial Services Authority and within the jurisdiction of the Financial Ombudsman Service and the Financial Services Compensation Scheme. There is a complaints procedure, details of which can be found in the terms and conditions. Calls may be monitored and recorded.

Foreword

Transport and Environment Committee

Dear Blue Badge Guide User

Welcome to the revised Association of London Government's Guide to parking in London for Blue Badge holders. We hope you enjoy the new format which should be easier to use than the previous map-style guide and which should enable Blue Badge holders to make full use of the parking concessions available to them in the London area.

London is a large and diverse city with a multitude of parking controls and restrictions. Holders of the Blue Badge can take advantage of concessions on most, but not all, of these and this guide aims to explain what the concessions are and where they apply.

Parking in central London, where traffic levels are much higher, causes its own particular problems and so the guide contains a comprehensive map of Central London, whose pages contain full details of the local parking rules for Blue Badge holders.

In addition to the central London map there are notes on using the Blue Badge throughout the rest of London and local information and some other maps for all the London councils as well as information about using your Blue Badge at London's airports.

I hope you enjoy this new improved guide. If you have any comments please use the feedback section at the end of the guide.

Yours,

Nick Lester

Director of Transport & Environment
Association of London Government

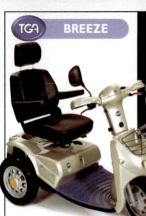

BREEZE
- Active, adjustable suspension
- Up to 30 miles on 1 charge
- Climbs hills with ease

SUPERLIGHT
- Very comfortable
- Carries up to 17 stone

FRONTIER
- Very comfortable
- Carries up to 25 stone
- Travel up to 25 miles

STRATA 3
- Folds away easily into boot of car
- Carries up to 16 stone
- Travel up to 12 miles

BETTER scooters BETTER prices!

"For over 25 years I've scoured the world to find the very best machines, at the lowest prices."

David Stone - Managing Director

At TGA we know more about scooters than anyone else in the UK. We'll help you go where you like, whenever you like - reliably, comfortably and safely.

BHTA - British Healthcare Trades Association

NOW AVAILABLE ON THE **Motability** SCHEME

For more details or home demonstration
CALL 0800 849 2064
Quote ref: LB0102C

TGA, Woodhall Business Park, Sudbury, Suffolk CO10 1WH.
Or visit our website www.tga-electric.com

THE MOST COMPREHENSIVE RANGE OF MOBILITY PRODUCTS IN THE UK AT ABSOLUTELY THE BEST PRICES!

☐ Please send me more information on the TGA range
☐ Please call to arrange a FREE home demonstration

Name ....
Telephone ....
Address ....
....
....
Postcode ....

Send to: TGA, Woodhall Business Park, Sudbury, Suffolk CO10 1WH.

LB0102C

Editor's Notes
Introduction to London Blue Badge Parking Guide.

This Guide is a new concept in community mapping. You will see that the Guide is fundamentally a London Street Atlas. The key difference is we have designed this with the Blue Badge driver in mind. We asked all 33 London Boroughs about their parking restrictions for Blue Badge holders and have presented this information using different background colours on the map. These colours reflect the parking concessions available to Blue Badge holders across London. We believe the concept is straightforward to use: simply locate where you want to go and the base background colour will show you which of the various on-street parking concessions apply in this area.

The Bays We have surveyed and marked out all Blue Badge Bays across London as well as the permitted bays on the Red Routes. In doing so, we have discovered that Blue Badge holders are permitted to park between the standard restriction times (i.e. 10am to 4pm) on the conventional **Red Route Parking Box bays**. These are different to Red Route Loading bays where you often see a Blue Badge sign typically with a maximum stay of 3 hours. Red Route parking box bays do not have any Blue Badge symbols yet you are permitted to park there for most of the day.

This information has been validated by TfL and is particularly good news in the central London area where you are only permitted to park in Blue Badge bays. Again these are all marked on the map.

Other useful information

We have also surveyed all car parks and petrol stations in London to determine accessibility of car parks and whether a petrol station offers Service Call. You will see from the key to symbols we have had to create a new range of symbols which I hope are straightforward. For car parks, the key criteria are:

1 Accessibility category 1, 2 or 3 (where 1 is the most accessible and 3 is the least accessible)

2 Any height restriction below 2.20m has a bar at the top of the symbol

3 Free or discounted parking for Blue Badge holders has a 'D' instead of the 'P' as the car park symbol

You will see we have constructed the symbols accordingly.

I hope you find the Guide of value and useful day to day. Please let me know if there's anything else you would like included in these maps.

Thanks… and keep on moving.
Freddie

The leading car scheme for disabled people

dreaming of a new car?

it's cheaper and easier than you think!

> *You can get a brand new car by simply using your Higher Rate Mobility Component of the Disability Living Allowance or War Pensioners' Mobility Supplement*

Every day, Motability helps thousands of disabled people and their families drive away in new cars. And, because we take care of the practicalities, you're free to enjoy affordable, convenient and worry-free motoring.

To find out more, call Motability on:
Freephone 0800 093 1000 or visit **www.motability.co.uk**

Registered Charity No: 299745

Introducing the Gowrings Mobility range of mobility solutions...

As the UK's leading manufacturer of cars adapted for wheelchair users travelling as passengers, we work hard to make your life easier. Whether it is a wheelchair passenger vehicle, a swivel seat, or a 4 IN 4 power chair, we offer friendly and professional mobility advice, a FREE UK-wide no-obligation demonstration, a dedicated after sales team and a 3 year warranty for your peace of mind.

gowrings mobility

For more information or to book a free, home demonstration
Lo-Call 0845 608 8020
www.gowringsmobility.co.uk

Please send me a full information pack to:

Mr/Mrs/Miss _____ First Name _____
Surname _____
Address _____
_____
Post Code _____
Home Telephone _____
Please post your coupon to:
Gowrings Mobility, FREEPOST, Newbury, Berkshire, RG14 5ZW

Wheelchair Passenger Vehicles • Swivel Seats • Power Chairs • Mobility Advice

The Blue Badge Scheme offers special parking concessions for some people with disabilities. It allows badge holders to park close to their destination. The concessions typically apply only to on street parking but some concessions apply in select Car Parks. This Guide illustrates the various concessions across London and will detail the specific on street parking options as well as detailing any other concession available close to your destination.

Blue Badge holders are entitled to parking concessions in other EU member states, and in some other European countries. A useful leaflet is available from Department for Transport that explains the concessions and lists all the countries.

On-street parking concessions

Listed below are the various on-street parking options for Blue Badge Holders. As you may already be aware some of the concessions vary across the London Boroughs. This Guide intends to illustrate based on your destination point what the on-street parking concession are. The on-street parking options include;

Red Route Box Bays

Red Routes mark out London's important roads identified by the red no-stopping lines or signs along the route. No stopping is permitted on these routes. Red boxes marked on the road indicate that parking, or loading is permitted during the off peak times, normally between 10am and 4 pm. Special conditions apply to Blue Badge Holders, typically a maximum of 3 hours. Ensure you check this time limit and try not to use these during the rush hours.

Single & double Yellow Lines

A Blue Badge Holder is permitted to park on single or double yellow lines in most areas up to 3 hours typically except where loading restrictions apply. You must ensure you are not causing an obstruction. Use your clock to indicate your arrival time.

Pay & display or metered parking

Payment for parking on Pay & Display or meters (where they still exist) does apply in some areas within London. Certain Borough's provide a period of time free of charge once an initial payment has been made. Please note Pay & Display machines often do not give any information on the concessions for Blue Badge Holders. Yet they do indicate which Borough they belong to. Either use the maps background colour coding to assess if parking on Pay & Display is permitted or refer to the table on page 80 and 81. Please note if your disability prevents you reaching the slot to put your money in you will need to write to the council to explain this if you get a ticket.

Blue Badge parking bays

You may park without time restriction in free parking bays which have a maximum stay, unless the signs show a time limit.

Residents Parking

Residents' parking provides the largest area of parking spaces within London and is readily distributed across most areas. Not all residents' spaces are free to use for Blue Badge Holders. Use the maps background colour coding to assess if parking in Residents parking Bays is permitted at your destination point.

Shared Used Bay

Shared use bays in some Boroughs are a combination of Pay & Display as well as residents parking. London Borough of Redbridge is the tricky one where you are permitted to park in Pay & Display but not in Residents and Shared Used bays. Use the map

background colour to assess if parking in Shared Used Bays is permitted at your destination point.

Where NOT to park
Red Routes

Red Routes prohibit parking for Blue Badge holders within the controlling hours. You can only stop briefly to set down or pick up the badge holder. Stopping to set down other non-disabled passengers is not permitted. Taxi's are also permitted to drop down and pick up on Red Routes. There are loading and parking bays available on these routes for parking please check the signs for times.

Loading Bans

Loading bans are shown by a single or double stripe on the kerb. Please ensure you do not park here. You are permitted to pick up or set down a passenger. Loading bans in London are typically on junctions, corners and the entrance or exit of streets. The double stripes indicate no loading at any time yet the single stripe should have a post mounted plate indicating the times no loading/unloading is permitted. If there is an arrow on the sign, it indicates the direction prohibition starts.

Pedestrian Areas

Please note in pedestrian areas, waiting and loading restrictions may be in force even where there are no yellow lines shown on the road or stripes on the kerb. The restrictions in force should be shown on plates displayed at the kerbside. This map has highlighted most of the pedestrian streets as well as the streets used for markets.

Clearways

Some areas are protected by clearway restrictions at certain times (check the plate) On clearways stopping is not permitted and there is no concession for Blue Badge Holders.

Double White Lines in the centre of the road

Should there be solid double white lines or even broken white lines you are typically not permitted to parking on that street.

Others areas NOT permitted to park include;

- Bus Lanes and Bus Stops during the hours of operation
- Cycle Lanes or pavements, footways or verges (except in areas where there are signs showing it is legal).
- On any pedestrian crossing which includes Zebra, Pelican, Toucan (for bicycles) and Puffin crossings.
- Next to any dropped footway either across a driveway or where the kerb has been lowered for pedestrians to cross.
- On zig-zag markings used typically before and after pedestrian crossings or school entrances and on markings where is it is written **KEEP CLEAR**.
- Blue Badge rules do **NOT** often apply at airports - see airport section for parking options.

Other Bays types NOT permitted to park

Do not park in suspended bays (shown by a yellow no parking sign or cones) or business, trader, doctor, police, diplomat, ambulance, motorcycle, or similar bays including taxi ranks.

Blue Badge Holders are not permitted to use dedicated disabled badge holder bays (indicated by a sign or painted on the street), often with a permit number painted by it.

Local Badge Schemes in Central London

You may be aware that within Central London the following boroughs have their registered disabled badge scheme for residents as well as their business residents; Westminster (white badge), Corporation of London (red badge), Kensington and Chelsea (purple badge) and Camden (green badge). These bays have not been marked on the map as they are typically assigned. The background mapping colour will help you determine which on-street options you are permitted to park on within these boroughs.

Hazardous places to even think about parking:

You must also ensure you do **NOT** park where it would be obstructive or cause danger to others. For example:

- On a bend in a road
- Near the brow of a hill
- Hump back bridge
- Close to junctions where it would make it difficult for others to see clearly
- By a traffic island, road works etc. where you would make the road much narrower
- Blocking vehicle entrances, particularly emergency vehicles

Important to know

Your vehicle cannot legally be wheel clamped on the public highway for parking offences provided a valid Blue Badge is correctly displayed. Be aware that if you park improperly on privately owned land you may risk having your vehicle clamped. If you park where it would cause an obstruction or be a danger to other road users your vehicle could be removed. You could also be prosecuted and your badge withdrawn.

What to do if?

Blue Badge Gets Stolen – report the theft immediately to the Police. The crime reference is likely to be required before a replacement badge can be issued.

Towed away or clamped – If your Blue Badge is displayed you should not be clamped or towed away even if you park illegally. If the vehicle is causing an obstruction it may be repositioned, but usually to a nearby street.

Car is missing – If your vehicle is missing call the TRACE service **020 7747 4747** (24 hours). They will be able to confirm if it has been towed away and where it has removed to.

You get a Parking Ticket (Penalty Charge Notices - PCN) – do not ignore it. You may have to pay more if you do not either pay or contest the ticket promptly. If you want to contest the ticket write to the council concerned.

Fixed Penalty Notices (FPN) are issued by the Police. If you want to contest the ticket you must ask for a court hearing by typically writing to the address on the back of the ticket.

Your duties as a Badge Holder

It is your responsibility to ensure that the badge is used properly. It is in your own interest that the badge should retain the respect of other motorists. Please play your part.

Do not allow others to use your Blue Badge – this is a criminal offence. To reduce the risk of this happening accidentally, you should remove the badge whenever you are not using the parking concessions.

You must ensure that the details on the front of the badge remain legible. If they become unreadable, the badge must be returned to the local authority to be re-issued.

 Ensure you set your clock and display your badge and clock clearly.

Visit **www.parkingforbluebadges.com** for our online mapping and information guide

Key to map pages

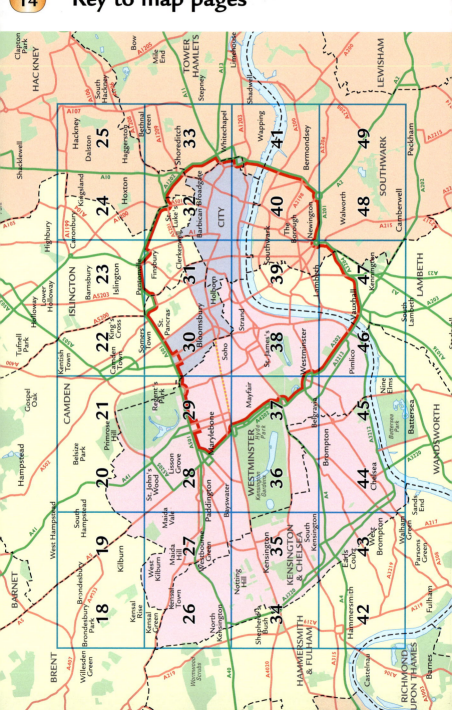

London Borough map 15

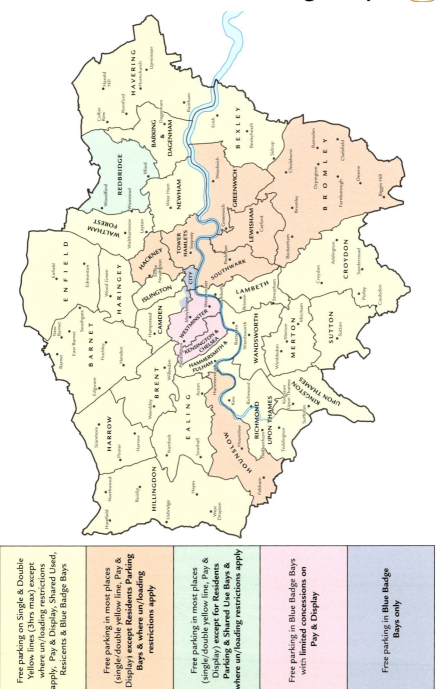

Key to map symbols

Dual **A4**	Primary Route
Dual **A40**	'A' Road
B504	'B' Road
	Other Road/Toll
A4	Red Route
	Street Market
	Restricted Access Road
	Pedestrian Street
	Cycle Path
-------	Track/Footpath
→	One Way Street
	Congestion zone
•	Statue/Memorial/Bandstand
	Leisure & Tourism
	Administration & Law
	Industry & Commerce
†	Cemetery
	Golf Course
	Public Open Space
	Wood/Forest
⇌	Main Railway Station
⊖	Other Railway Station
⊖	London Underground Station
⊖	Docklands Light Railway Station
⊖	Light Railway Station
⊖	Bus/Coach Station

Colours refer to the background colour of the mapping. Also see page 15.

Free parking on Single & Double Yellow lines (3hrs max) except where un/loading restrictions apply, Pay & Display, Shared Used, Residents & Blue Badge Bays

Free parking in most places (single/double yellow line, Pay & Display) **except Residents Parking Bays & where un/loading restrictions apply**

Free parking in most places (single/double yellow line, Pay & Display) **except for Residents Parking & Shared Use Bays & where un/loading restrictions apply**

Free parking in Blue Badge Bays with **limited concessions on Pay & Display**

Free parking in **Blue Badge Bays only**

Shopmobility

Petrol station

Petrol station with service call

Petrol station with accessible toilet for the disabled

Petrol station with service call with accessible toilet for the disabled

Wheelchair accessible public toilet

On Street Parking

Blue Badge parking bay

Red Route box bay

Character within circle refers to parking duration e.g.

3 - 3 hours **4** - 4 hours

U - unlimited **!** - check signs locally

Off Street Parking

Car park

Car park free or discounted for Blue Badge holders

Car park with height restriction of 2.20m or less

Car park with height restrictions free or discounted for Blue Badge holders

Car park with height restrictions free or discounted for Blue Badge holders. Weekends only

Coach park

Number within square refers to the accessibility of the car park eg:

D1 is a car park discounted for Blue Badge holder, accessible to a wheelchair-user travelling independently

Definition of accessibility grading used for car parks

 1 - Accessible to a wheelchair-user travelling independently

 2 - Accessible to a wheelchair-user travelling with assistance

 3 - Accessible to a wheelchair-user or someone with limited mobility, able to walk a few paces and up a max of three steps

SCALE 1:13,000

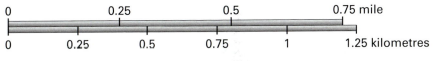

4.9 inches to 1 mile/7.7 cm to 1 km

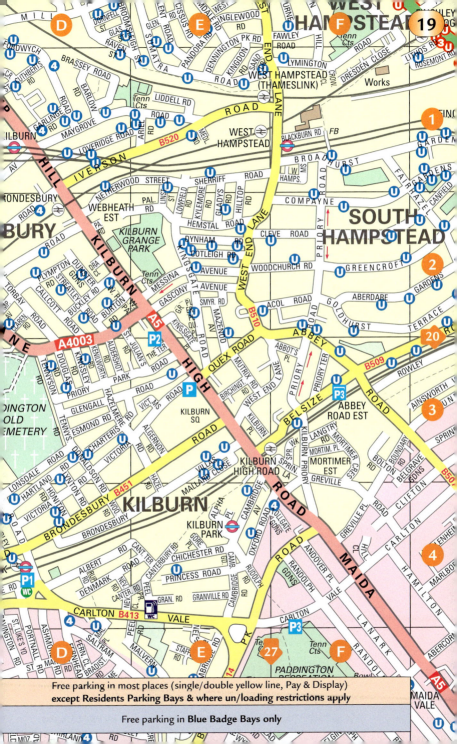

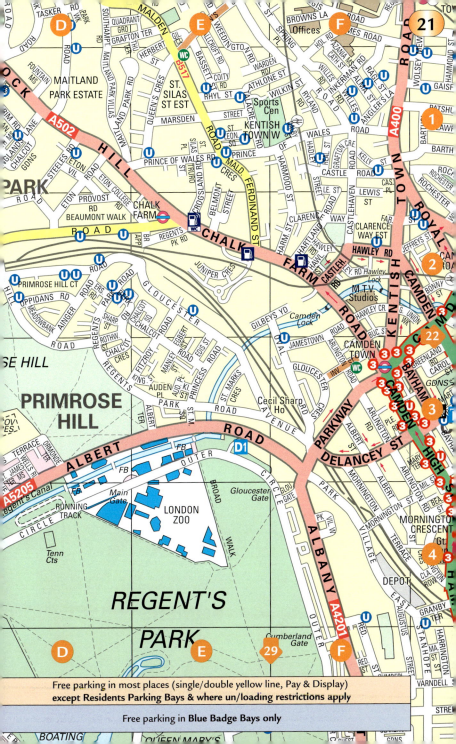

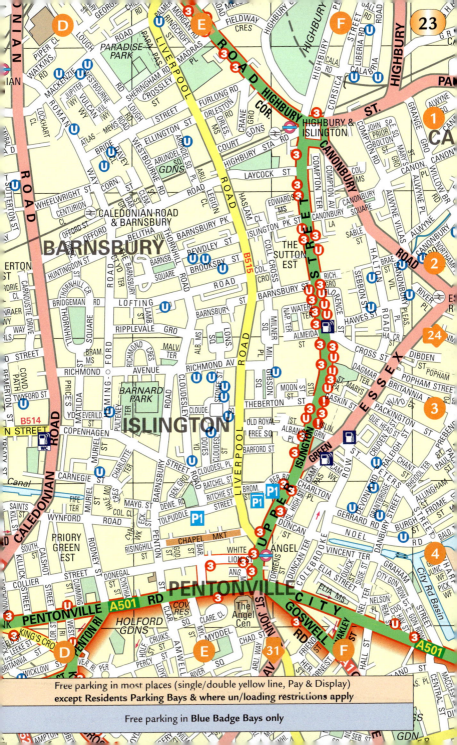

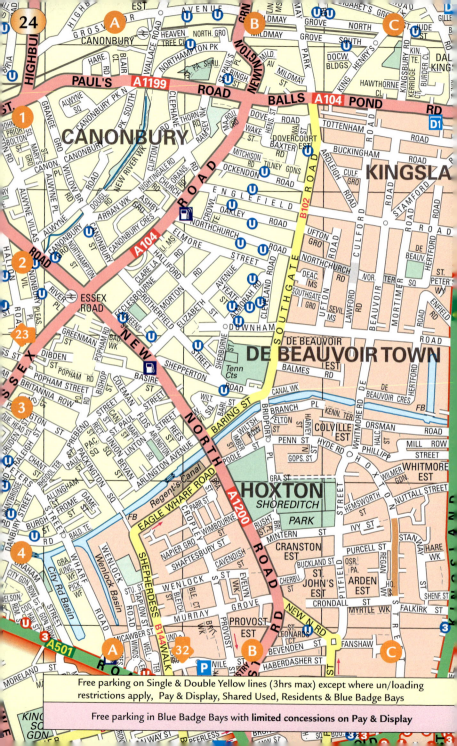

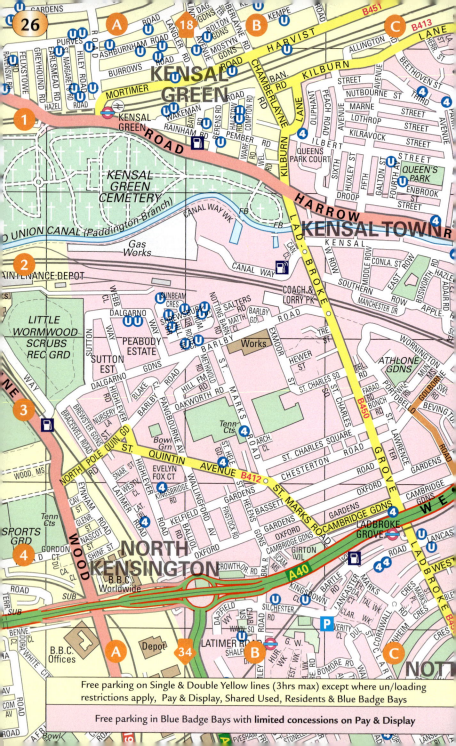

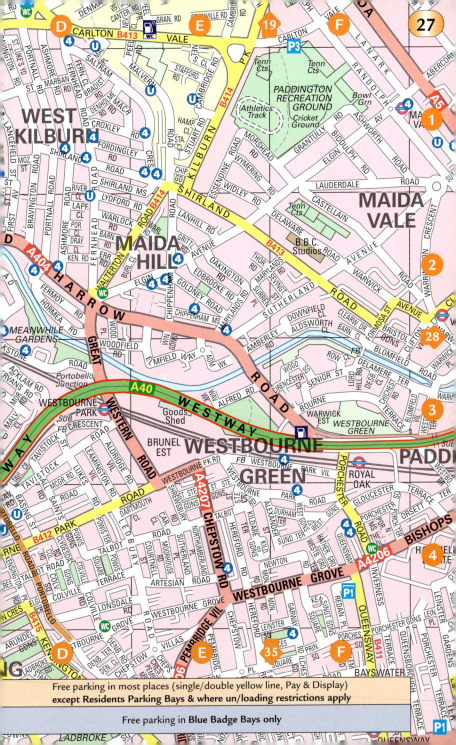

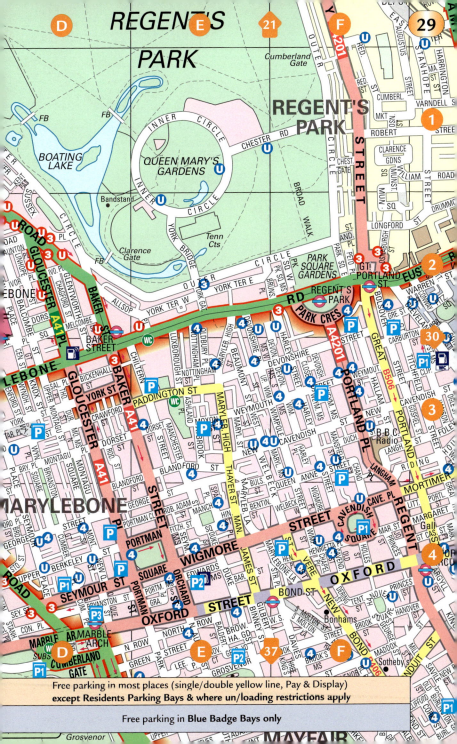

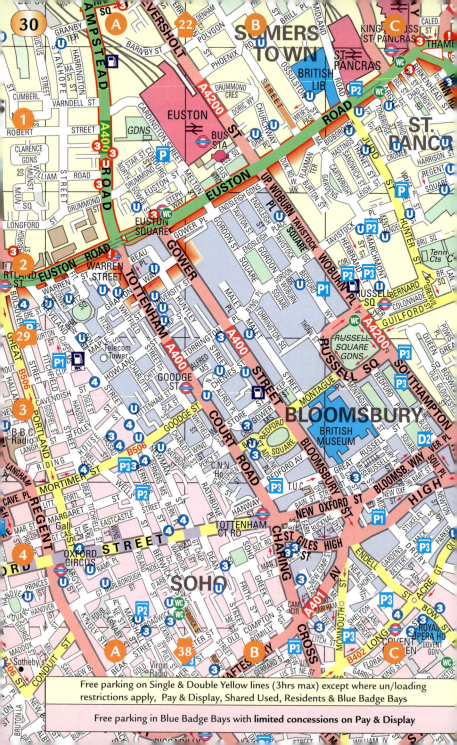

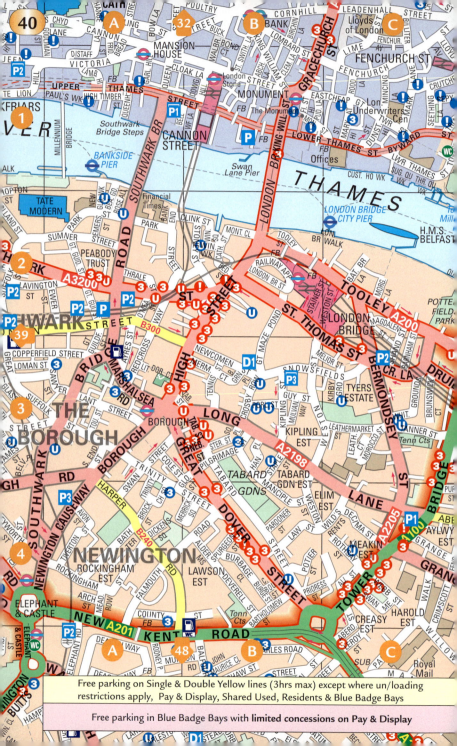

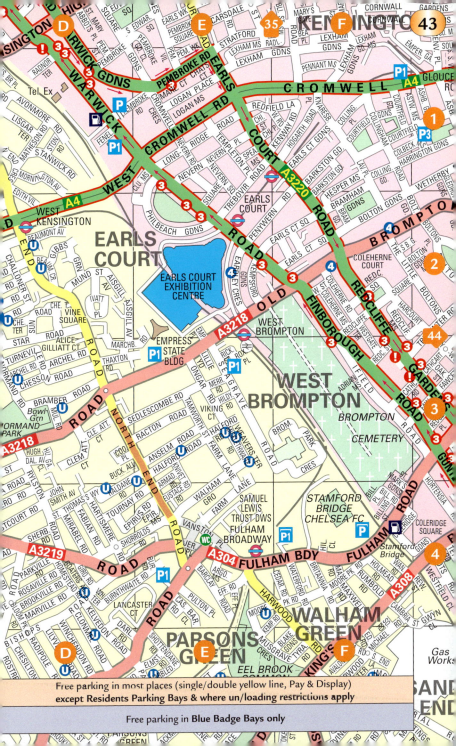

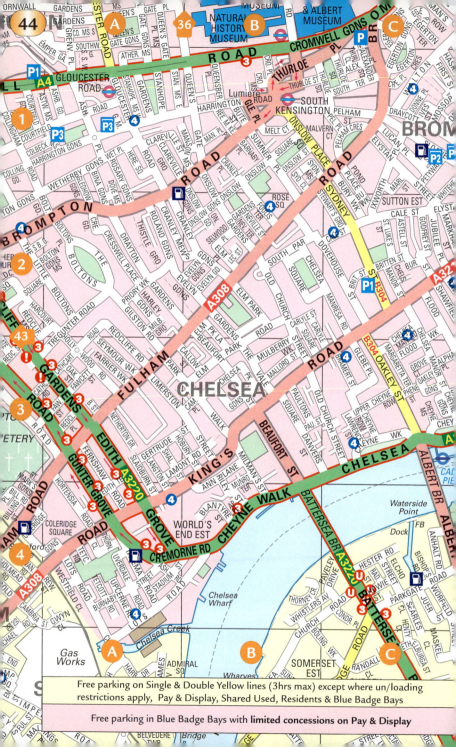

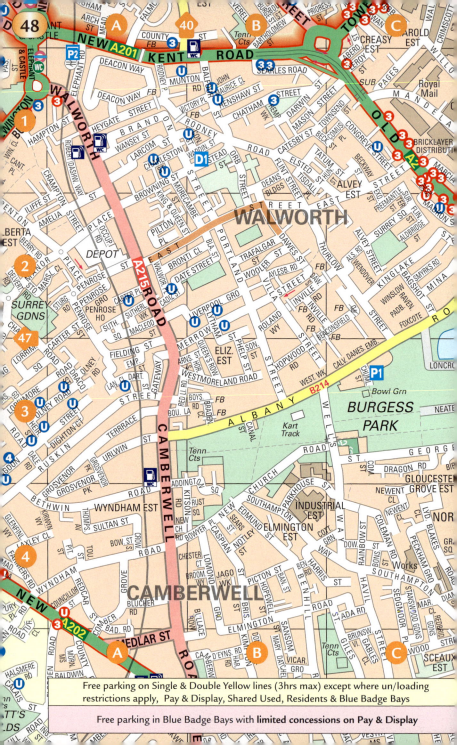

INDEX TO STREET NAMES

General Abbreviations

All	Alley	Dws	Dwellings	Hts	Heights	Ri	Rise
App	Approach	E	East	Ind	Industrial	S	South
Arc	Arcade	Embk	Embankment	Junct	Junction	Sch	School
Av	Avenue	Est	Estate	La	Lane	Shop	Shopping
Bdy	Broadway	Ex	Exchange	Lo	Lodge	Sq	Square
Bldgs	Buildings	Fld	Field	Mans	Mansions	St.	Saint
Br	Bridge	Flds	Fields	Mkt	Market	St	Street
Cen	Central, Centre	Fm	Farm	Mkts	Markets	Sta	Station
Ch	Church	Gdn	Garden	Ms	Mews	Ter	Terrace
Chyd	Churchyard	Gdns	Gardens	Mt	Mount	Trd	Trading
Circ	Circus	Gra	Grange	N	North	Twr	Tower
Cl	Close	Grd	Ground	Par	Parade	Vil	Villas
Cor	Corner	Grds	Grounds	Pas	Passage	Vw	View
Cotts	Cottages	Grn	Green	Pk	Park	W	West
Cres	Crescent	Gro	Grove	Pl	Place	Wd	Wood
Ct	Court	Gt	Great	Prec	Precinct	Wf	Wharf
Ctyd	Courtyard	Ho	House	Pt	Point	Wk	Walk
Dr	Drive	Hos	Houses	Rd	Road	Yd	Yard

Notes
The figures and letters following a street name indicate the Postal District, page and map square where the name can be found.

A

Name	Page	Sq
Abbey Gdns NW8	20	A4
Abbey Gdns W6	42	C3
Abbey Orchard St SW1	38	B4
Abbey Rd NW6	19	F2
Abbey Rd NW8	20	A4
Abbey Rd Est NW8	19	F3
Abbey St SE1	40	C4
Abbotsbury Rd W14	34	C3
Abbots Manor Est SW1	45	F1
Abbot's Pl NW6	19	F3
Abbot St E8	25	D1
Abchurch La EC4	40	B1
Abercorn Cl NW8	28	A1
Abercorn Pl NW8	28	A1
Abercorn Way SE1	49	E2
Aberdare Gdns NW6	19	F2
Aberdeen Pl NW8	28	B2
Aberdour St SE1	48	C1
Abingdon Rd W8	35	E4
Abingdon St SW1	38	C4
Abingdon Vil W8	35	E4
Acacia Pl NW8	20	B4
Acacia Rd NW8	20	B4
Acanthus Dr SE1	49	E2
Achilles Cl SE1	49	E2
Acklam Rd W10	27	D3
Acol Rd NW6	19	E2
Acton Ms E8	25	D3
Acton St WC1	31	D1
Adair Rd W10	26	C2
Adam & Eve Ms W8	35	F4
Adamson Rd NW3	20	B2
Adams Row W1	37	E1
Adam St WC2	38	C1
Adam Wk SW6	42	A4
Ada Pl E2	25	E3
Ada Rd SE5	48	C4
Ada St E8	25	F3
Addington Sq SE5	48	A4
Addison Av W11	34	C2
Addison Br Pl W14	43	D1
Addison Cres W14	34	C4
Addison Gdns W14	34	B4
Addison Pl W11	34	C2
Addison Rd W14	35	D4
Adelaide Rd NW3	20	B2
Adeline Pl WC1	30	B3
Adeney Cl W6	42	B3
Adie Rd W6	34	A4
Adler St E1	33	E4
Admiral Wk W9	27	E3
Adpar St W2	28	B2
Adrian Ms SW10	43	F3
Africa Ho SE16	41	F4
Agar Gro NW1	22	A2
Agar Gro Est NW1	22	B2
Agar Pl NW1	22	A2
Agar St WC2	38	C1
Agate Rd W6	34	A4
Agdon St EC1	31	F2
Ainger Rd NW3	21	D2
Ainsdale Dr SE1	49	E2
Ainsley St E2	33	F1
Ainsworth Way NW8	20	A3
Aintree St SW6	42	C4
Airdrie Cl N1	23	D2
Airlie Gdns W8	35	E3
Air St W1	38	A1
Aisgill Av W14	43	D2
Albany Mans SW11	44	C4
Albany Rd SE5	48	B3
Albany St NW1	21	F4
Albemarle St W1	37	F1
Alberta Est SE17	47	F2
Alberta St SE17	47	F2
Albert Av SW8	47	D4
Albert Br SW3	44	C3
Albert Br SW11	44	C3
Albert Br Rd SW11	44	C4
Albert Embk SE1	46	C2
Albert Gate SW1	37	D3
Albert Pl W8	35	F3
Albert Rd NW6	19	D4
Albert Sq SW8	47	D4
Albert St NW1	21	F3
Albert Ter NW1	21	E3
Albert Way SE15	49	F4
Albion Dr E8	25	D2
Albion Ms N1	23	E3
Albion Ms W2	28	C4
Albion Pl EC1	31	F3
Albion Sq E8	25	D2
Albion St W2	28	C4
Albion Ter E8	25	D2
Aldbridge St SE17	48	C2
Aldebert Ter SW8	46	C4
Aldenham St NW1	22	B4
Alder Cl SE15	49	D3
Aldermanbury EC2	32	A4
Alderney Ms SE1	40	B4
Alderney St SW1	45	F1
Aldersgate St EC1	32	A3
Aldershot Rd NW6	19	D3
Aldford St W1	37	E2
Aldgate EC3	32	C4
Aldgate High St EC3	33	D4
Aldine St W12	34	A3
Aldridge Rd Vil W11	27	D3
Aldsworth Cl W9	27	F2
Aldwych WC2	39	D1
Alexander Pl SW7	44	C1
Alexander Sq SW3	44	C1
Alexander St W2	27	E4
Alexandra Pl NW8	20	A3
Alexandra Rd NW8	20	A2
Alexis St SE16	49	F1
Alfred Ms W1	30	B3
Alfred Pl WC1	30	B3
Alfred Rd W2	27	E3
Algernon Rd NW6	19	E3
Alice Gilliatt Ct W14	43	D3
Alice St SE1	40	C4
Alie St E1	33	D4
Allensbury Pl NW1	22	B2
Allen St W8	35	E4
Allestree Rd SW6	42	C4
Allingham St N1	24	A4
Allington Rd W10	18	C4

All-Bar 51

Name	Page	Grid
Allington St SW1	37	F4
Allitsen Rd NW8	20	C4
All Saints Rd W11	27	D3
All Saints St N1	23	D4
Allsop Pl NW1	29	D2
Alma Gro SE1	49	D1
Alma Sq NW8	28	A1
Alma St NW5	21	F1
Almeida St N1	23	F2
Almond Rd SE16	49	F1
Almorah Rd N1	24	B2
Alperton St W10	26	C2
Alpha Pl NW6	19	E4
Alpha Pl SW3	44	C3
Alsace Rd SE17	48	C2
Alscot Rd SE1	49	D1
Alscot Way SE1	49	D1
Alverstone Rd NW2	18	A2
Alvey Est SE17	48	C1
Alvey St SE17	48	C2
Alwyne Pl N1	24	A1
Alwyne Rd N1	24	A2
Alwyne Sq N1	24	A1
Alwyne Vil N1	23	F2
Ambergate St SE17	47	F2
Amberley Rd W9	27	E3
Ambrosden Av SW1	38	A4
Ambrose St SE16	49	F1
Amelia St SE17	47	F2
Amor Rd W6	34	A4
Ampton St WC1	31	D1
Amwell St EC1	31	E1
Anchor St SE16	49	F1
Ancill Cl W6	42	C3
Anderson St SW3	45	D2
Andover Rd N7	19	F4
Andrew's Rd E8	25	F3
Angel Ct EC2	32	B4
Angel Ms N1	23	E4
Angel St EC1	32	A4
Angel Wk W6	42	A1
Angler's La NW5	21	F1
Angrave Ct E8	25	D3
Anhalt Rd SW11	44	C4
Anley Rd W14	34	B3
Anna Cl E8	25	D3
Ann La SW10	44	B4
Ansdell St W8	35	F4
Anselm Rd SW6	43	E3
Ansleigh Pl W11	34	B1
Antrim Gro NW3	21	D1
Antrim Mans NW3	20	C1
Antrim Rd NW3	21	D1
Apollo Pl SW10	44	B4
Appleby Rd E8	25	E2
Appleby St E2	25	D4
Appleford Rd W10	26	C2
Applegarth Rd W14	34	B4
Appold St EC2	32	C3
Aquila St NW8	20	B4
Arbutus St E8	24	C3
Archel Rd W14	43	D3
Archery Cl W2	28	C4
Archibald Ms W1	37	E1
Arch St SE1	40	A4
Archway Cl W10	26	B3
Arden Est N1	24	C4
Ardleigh Rd N1	24	B1
Argon Ms SW6	43	E4
Argyle Sq WC1	30	C1
Argyle St WC1	30	C1
Argyle Way SE16	49	E2
Argyll Rd W8	35	E3
Argyll St W1	30	A4
Ariel Rd NW6	19	E1
Ariel Way W12	34	A2
Arlington Av N1	24	A4
Arlington Rd NW1	21	F3
Arlington Sq N1	24	A3
Arlington St SW1	38	A2
Arlington Way EC1	31	E1
Armadale Rd SW6	43	E4
Armstrong Rd SW7	36	B4
Arne St WC2	30	C4
Arnold Circ E2	33	D1
Arnold Est SE1	41	D3
Arnside St SE17	48	A3
Arran Wk N1	24	A2
Artesian Rd W2	27	E4
Artillery La E1	32	C3
Artillery Row SW1	38	B4
Arundel Gdns W11	35	D1
Arundel Pl N1	23	E1
Arundel Sq N7	23	E1
Arundel St WC2	39	D1
Ascalon St SW8	46	A4
Ashbridge St NW8	28	C2
Ashburn Gdns SW7	44	A1
Ashburnham Rd NW10	26	A1
Ashburnham Rd SW10	44	A4
Ashburn Pl SW7	44	A1
Ashby Gro N1	24	A2
Asher Way E1	41	E2
Ashfield St E1	33	F3
Ash Gro E8	25	F3
Ashland Pl W1	29	E3
Ashley Gdns SW1	38	A4
Ashley Pl SW1	38	A4
Ashmill St NW1	28	C3
Ashmole Pl SW8	47	D3
Ashmole St SW8	47	D3
Ashmore Rd W9	27	D2
Ashwin St E8	25	D1
Ashworth Rd W9	27	F1
Aspenlea Rd W6	42	B3
Aspinden Rd SE16	49	F1
Astell St SW3	44	C2
Astrop Ms W6	34	A4
Astrop Ter W6	34	A4
Astwood Ms SW7	43	F1
Asylum Rd SE15	49	F4
Atherstone Ms SW7	44	A1
Athlone St NW5	21	E1
Atlas Ms N7	23	D1
Atterbury St SW1	46	B1
Aubrey Rd W8	35	D2
Aubrey Wk W8	35	D2
Auden Pl NW1	21	E3
Audrey St E2	25	E4
Augustine Rd W14	34	B4
Augustus St NW1	21	F4
Aulton Pl SE11	47	E2
Auriol Rd W14	42	C1
Austen Ho NW6	27	E1
Austin Friars EC2	32	B4
Austin St E2	33	D1
Austral St SE11	47	F1
Aveline St SE11	47	E2
Ave Maria La EC4	31	F4
Avenue, The NW6	18	B3
Avenue Cl NW8	20	C3
Avenue Rd NW3	20	B2
Avenue Rd NW8	20	B2
Averill St W6	42	B3
Avery Row W1	37	F1
Avondale Pk Gdns W11	34	C1
Avondale Pk Rd W11	34	C1
Avondale Sq SE1	49	E2
Avonmore Rd W14	43	D1
Avonmouth St SE1	40	A4
Aybrook St W1	29	E3
Aylesbury Rd SE17	48	B2
Aylesbury St EC1	31	F2
Aylesford St SW1	46	B2
Aylestone Av NW6	18	B3
Aylwyn Est SE1	40	C4
Aynhoe Rd W14	42	B1
Ayres St SE1	40	A3

B

Name	Page	Grid
Baches St N1	32	B1
Back Ch La E1	41	E1
Back Hill EC1	31	E2
Bacon Gro SE1	41	D4
Bacon St E1	33	D2
Bacon St E2	33	D2
Baddow Wk N1	24	A3
Badsworth Rd SE5	48	A4
Bagshot St SE17	48	C2
Bainbridge St WC1	30	B4
Baker's Row EC1	31	E2
Baker St NW1	29	D2
Baker St W1	29	D3
Balaclava Rd SE1	49	D1
Balcombe St NW1	29	D2
Balderton St W1	29	E4
Baldwin's Gdns EC1	31	E3
Baldwin Ter N1	24	A4
Balfe St N1	22	C4
Balfour St SE17	48	B1
Balliol Rd W10	26	A4
Balls Pond Rd N1	24	B1
Balmes Rd N1	24	B3
Balmoral Gro N7	23	D1
Balniel Gate SW1	46	B2
Baltic St E EC1	32	A2
Baltic St W EC1	32	A2
Balvaird Pl SW1	46	B2
Bamborough Gdns W12	34	A3
Banister Rd W10	26	B1
Bank End SE1	40	A2
Bannerman Ho SW8	47	D3
Banner St EC1	32	A2
Bantry St SE5	48	B4
Barandon Wk W11	34	B1
Barbican, The EC2	32	A3
Barb Ms W6	34	A4
Barclay Cl SW6	43	E4
Barclay Rd SW6	43	E4
Bard Rd W10	34	B1
Barfett St W10	27	D2
Barford St N1	23	E3
Baring St N1	24	B3
Barker Dr NW1	22	A2
Barker St SW10	44	A3
Bark Pl W2	35	F1
Barkston Gdns SW5	43	E4
Barkworth Rd SE16	49	F2
Barlby Gdns W10	26	B2
Barlby Rd W10	26	B2
Barlow Rd NW6	19	D1
Barnaby Pl SW7	44	B1
Barnby St NW1	22	A4
Barnet Gro E2	33	E1
Barnham St SE1	40	C3
Barnsbury Gro N7	23	D2
Barnsbury Pk N1	23	E2
Barnsbury Rd N1	23	E4
Barnsbury Sq N1	23	E2
Barnsbury St N1	23	E2
Barnsbury Ter N1	23	D2

Street	Page	Grid
Barnsdale Rd W9	27	D2
Barnsley St E1	33	F2
Barnwood Cl W9	27	F2
Barons Ct Rd W14	42	C2
Barons Keep W14	42	C2
Barons Pl SE1	39	E3
Baron St N1	23	E4
Barrett St W1	29	E4
Barrow Hill Rd NW8	20	C4
Barter St WC1	30	C3
Bartholomew Cl EC1	32	A3
Bartholomew Rd NW5	22	A1
Bartholomew Sq EC1	32	A2
Bartholomew St SE1	40	B4
Bartholomew Vil NW5	22	A1
Bartle Rd W11	26	C4
Barton Rd W14	42	C2
Basil St SW3	37	D4
Basinghall Av EC2	32	B3
Basinghall St EC2	32	A3
Basing St W11	27	D4
Basire St N1	24	A3
Bassett Rd W10	26	B4
Bassett St NW5	21	E1
Bastwick St EC1	31	F2
Batchelor St N1	23	E4
Bateman's Row EC2	32	C2
Bath EC1	32	B1
Bath Ter SE1	40	A4
Bathurst St W2	36	B1
Batoum Gdns W6	34	A4
Battersea Br SW3	44	B4
Battersea Br SW11	44	B4
Battersea Br Rd SW11	44	C4
Battersea Pk SW11	45	D4
Battle Br La SE1	40	C2
Battle Br Rd NW1	22	C4
Batty St E1	33	E4
Baxendale St E2	33	E1
Baxter Rd N1	24	B1
Bayford Rd NW10	26	B1
Bayford St E8	25	F2
Bayham Pl NW1	22	A3
Bayham St NW1	22	A3
Bayley St WC1	30	B3
Baylis Rd SE1	39	E3
Baynes St NW1	22	A2
Bayonne Rd W6	42	C3
Bayswater Rd W2	36	B1
Beaconsfield Rd SE17	48	B2
Beaconsfield Ter Rd W14	34	C4
Beadon Rd W6	42	A1
Beak St W1	38	A1
Bear Gdns SE1	40	A2
Bear La SE1	39	F2
Beatrice Pl W8	35	F4
Beatrice Rd SE1	49	E1
Beatty St NW1	22	A4
Beauchamp Pl SW3	36	C4
Beaufort Gdns SW3	36	C4
Beaufort St SW3	44	B3
Beaufoy Wk SE11	47	D1
Beaumont Av W14	43	D2
Beaumont Cres W14	43	D2
Beaumont Pl W1	30	A2
Beaumont St W1	29	E3
Beaumont Wk NW3	21	D2
Beck Rd E8	25	F3
Beckway St SE17	48	B1
Bedale St SE1	40	B2
Bedford Av WC1	30	B3
Bedford Gdns W8	35	E2
Bedford Pl WC1	30	C3
Bedford Row WC1	31	D3
Bedford Sq WC1	30	B3
Bedford St WC2	38	C1
Bedford Way WC1	30	B2
Beech St EC2	32	A3
Beechwood Rd E8	25	D1
Beehive Cl E8	25	D2
Beeston Pl SW1	37	F4
Beethoven St W10	26	C1
Belgrave Gdns NW8	19	F3
Belgrave Ms N SW1	37	E4
Belgrave Ms S SW1	37	E4
Belgrave Ms W SW1	37	E4
Belgrave Pl SW1	37	E4
Belgrave Rd SW1	45	F1
Belgrave Sq SW1	37	E4
Belgrove St WC1	30	C1
Belitha Vil N1	23	D2
Bell La E1	33	D3
Bell St NW1	28	C3
Bell Wf La EC4	40	A1
Bell Yd WC2	31	E4
Belmont St NW1	21	E2
Belsize Av NW3	20	B1
Belsize Gro NW3	20	C1
Belsize La NW3	20	B1
Belsize Pk NW3	20	B1
Belsize Pk Gdns NW3	20	C1
Belsize Rd NW6	19	F3
Belsize Sq NW3	20	B1
Belsize Ter NW3	20	B1
Belvedere Pl SE1	39	F3
Belvedere Rd SE1	39	D2
Bembridge Cl NW6	18	C2
Bemerton Est N1	23	D3
Bemerton St N1	23	D3
Benhill Rd SE5	48	B4
Benjamin Cl E8	25	E3
Benjamin St EC1	31	F3
Bentinck St W1	29	E4
Berens Rd NW10	26	B1
Berkeley Sq W1	37	F1
Berkeley St W1	37	F1
Berkley Rd NW1	21	D2
Bermondsey St SE1	40	C3
Bermondsey Wall E SE16	41	E3
Bermondsey Wall W SE16	41	E3
Bernard St WC1	30	C2
Berners Ms W1	30	A3
Berners Pl W1	30	A4
Berners Rd N1	23	E4
Berners St W1	30	A3
Bernhardt Cres NW8	28	C2
Berryfield Rd SE17	47	F2
Berry St EC1	31	F2
Berwick St W1	30	A4
Beryl Rd W6	42	B2
Bessborough Gdns SW1	46	B2
Bessborough Pl SW1	46	B2
Bessborough St SW1	46	B2
Bethnal Grn Rd E1	33	D2
Bethnal Grn Rd E2	33	D2
Bethwin Rd SE5	47	F4
Betterton St WC2	30	C4
Bevan St N1	24	A3
Bevenden St N1	32	B1
Bevington Rd W10	26	C3
Bevington St SE16	41	E3
Bevis Marks EC3	32	C4
Bewdley St N1	23	E2
Bewick Ms SE15	49	F4
Bianca Rd SE15	49	D3
Bibury Cl SE15	48	C3
Bickenhall St W1	29	D3
Bidborough St WC1	30	B1
Biddulph Rd W9	27	F1
Bigland St E1	33	F4
Billing Pl SW10	43	F4
Billing Rd SW10	43	F4
Billing St SW10	43	F4
Billiter St EC3	32	C4
Bina Gdns SW5	44	A1
Bingfield St N1	22	C3
Bingham St N1	24	B1
Binney St W1	29	E4
Birchington Rd NW6	19	E3
Birchin La EC3	32	B4
Birdcage Wk SW1	38	A3
Bird in Bush Rd SE15	49	E4
Birkbeck St E2	33	F1
Birkenhead St WC1	30	C1
Biscay Rd W6	42	B2
Bishop Kings Rd W14	42	C1
Bishops Br W2	28	A4
Bishops Br Rd W2	27	F4
Bishopsgate EC2	32	C4
Bishop's Rd SW11	44	C4
Bishops Ter SE11	47	E1
Bishop St N1	24	A3
Bishops Way E2	25	F4
Blackburne's Ms W1	37	E1
Blackburn Rd NW6	19	F1
Blackfriars Br EC4	39	F1
Blackfriars Br SE1	39	F1
Black Friars La EC4	39	F1
Blackfriars Rd SE1	39	F2
Blacklands Ter SW3	45	D1
Black Prince Rd SE1	47	D1
Black Prince Rd SE11	47	D1
Blackstone Est E8	25	F2
Blackwood St SE17	48	B2
Blagrove Rd W10	26	C3
Blair Cl N1	24	A1
Blake Cl W10	26	A3
Blakes Rd SE15	48	C4
Blanchard Way E8	25	E1
Blandford Sq NW1	28	C2
Blandford St W1	29	E3
Blantyre St SW10	44	B4
Blashford NW3	21	D2
Blenheim Cres W11	26	C4
Blenheim Rd NW8	20	A4
Blenheim Ter NW8	20	A4
Bletchley Ct N1	24	B4
Bletchley St N1	24	A4
Blithfield St W8	35	F4
Blomfield Rd W9	28	A3
Blomfield St EC2	32	B3
Blomfield Vil W2	27	F3
Bloomfield Pl W1	37	F1
Bloomfield Ter SW1	45	E2
Bloom Pk Rd SW6	43	D4
Bloomsbury Pl WC1	30	C3
Bloomsbury Sq WC1	30	C3
Bloomsbury St WC1	30	B3
Bloomsbury Way WC1	30	C4
Blossom St E1	32	C3
Blucher Rd SE5	48	A4
Blue Anchor La SE16	49	E1
Blue Anchor Yd E1	41	E1
Blundell St N7	22	C2
Blythe Rd W14	34	B4
Blythe St E2	33	F1
Boathouse Wk SE15	49	D4
Bocking St E8	25	F3
Bohemia Pl E8	25	F1
Bolingbroke Rd W14	34	B4

Bol-Bur 53

Name	Page	Grid
Bolingbroke Wk SW11	44	B4
Bolney St SW8	47	D4
Bolsover St W1	29	F2
Bolton Cres SE5	47	F3
Bolton Gdns NW10	18	B4
Bolton Gdns SW5	43	F2
Bolton Gdns Ms SW10	43	F2
Bolton Rd NW8	19	F3
Boltons, The SW10	44	A2
Boltons Pl SW5	44	A2
Bolton St W1	37	F2
Bombay St SE16	49	F1
Bomore Rd W11	34	B1
Bonar Rd SE15	49	E4
Bonchurch Rd W10	26	C3
Bond Ct EC4	32	B4
Bondway SW8	46	C3
Bonhill St EC2	32	B2
Bonnington Sq SW8	47	D3
Bonny St NW1	22	A2
Bonsor St SE5	48	C4
Boot St N1	32	C1
Borough High St SE1	40	A3
Borough Rd SE1	39	F4
Boscobel Pl SW1	45	E1
Boscobel St NW8	28	B2
Boston Pl NW1	29	D2
Boswell St WC1	30	C3
Bosworth Rd W10	26	C2
Boundary La SE17	48	A3
Boundary Rd NW8	19	F3
Boundary St E2	33	D2
Bourdon St W1	37	F1
Bourne Est EC1	31	E3
Bourne St SW1	45	E1
Bourne Ter W2	27	F3
Bouverie Pl W2	28	B4
Bouverie St EC4	31	E4
Bowden St SE11	47	E2
Bowfell Rd W6	42	A3
Bowhill Cl SW9	47	E4
Bow La EC4	32	A4
Bowl Ct EC2	32	C2
Bowling Grn La EC1	31	E2
Bowling Grn Pl SE1	40	B3
Bowling Grn St SE11	47	E3
Bow St WC2	30	C4
Bowyer Pl SE5	48	B4
Bowyer St SE5	48	A4
Boyd St E1	33	E4
Boyfield St SE1	39	F3
Boyne Ter Ms W11	35	D2
Boyson Rd SE17	48	B3
Bracewell Rd W10	26	A3
Bracklyn St N1	24	B4
Bradenham Cl SE17	48	B3
Bradiston Rd W9	27	D1
Bradmead SW8	45	F4
Brady St E1	33	F2
Braes St N1	23	F2
Braganza St SE17	47	F2
Braham St E1	33	D4
Braithwaite Twr W2	28	B3
Bramber Rd W14	43	D3
Bramerton St SW3	44	C3
Bramham Gdns SW5	43	F2
Bramley Rd W10	34	B1
Bramwell Ms N1	23	D3
Branch Pl N1	24	B3
Branch St SE15	48	C4
Brandon Est SE17	47	F3
Brandon Rd N7	22	C2
Brandon St SE17	48	A1
Brangton Rd SE11	47	D2
Branksea St SW6	42	C4
Brasenose Dr SW13	42	A3
Brassey Rd NW6	19	D1
Bravington Rd W9	19	D4
Bray NW3	20	C2
Bray Pl SW3	45	D1
Bread St EC4	40	A1
Bream's Bldgs EC4	31	E4
Brecon Rd W6	42	C3
Bremner Rd SW7	36	A3
Brendon St W1	28	C4
Brenthouse Rd E9	25	F2
Bressenden Pl SW1	37	F4
Brewer St W1	38	A1
Brewery Rd N7	22	C2
Brewhouse La E1	41	F2
Brewster Gdns W10	26	A3
Brick La E1	33	D3
Brick La E2	33	D1
Bricklayer's Arms Distribution Cen SE1	48	C1
Brick St W1	37	F2
Bride St N7	23	D1
Bridewain St SE1	41	D4
Bridge App NW1	21	E2
Bridge Av W6	42	A2
Bridgefoot SE1	46	C2
Bridgeman Rd N1	23	D2
Bridgeman St NW8	20	C4
Bridge Pl SW1	45	F1
Bridge St SW1	38	C3
Bridge Vw W6	42	A2
Bridgeway St NW1	22	A4
Bridport Pl N1	24	B4
Brill Pl NW1	22	B4
Brinklow Ho W2	27	F3
Brisbane St SE5	48	B4
Bristol Gdns W9	27	F2
Britannia Rd SW6	43	F4
Britannia Row N1	23	F3
Britannia St WC1	31	D1
Britannia Wk N1	32	B1
Britten St SW3	44	C2
Britton St EC1	31	F2
Broadfield La NW1	22	C2
Broadhurst Gdns NW6	19	F1
Broad La EC2	32	C3
Broadley St NW8	28	C3
Broadley Ter NW1	28	C2
Broad Sanctuary SW1	38	B3
Broad Wk NW1	29	F1
Broad Wk W1	37	E2
Broad Wk, The W8	35	F2
Broadwalk Ct W8	35	E2
Broadwall SE1	39	E2
Broadway SW1	38	B4
Broadway Mkt E8	25	F3
Broadwick St W1	30	A4
Brockham St SE1	40	A4
Broke Wk E8	25	E3
Bromfield St N1	23	E4
Brompton Pk Cres SW6	43	F3
Brompton Pl SW3	36	C4
Brompton Rd SW1	36	C4
Brompton Rd SW3	36	C4
Brompton Rd SW7	36	C4
Brompton Sq SW3	36	C4
Bromyard Ho SE15	49	F4
Brondesbury Ct NW2	18	A1
Brondesbury Pk NW6	18	B2
Brondesbury Rd NW6	19	D4
Brondesbury Vil NW6	19	D4
Bronsart Rd SW6	42	C4
Bronte Ho NW6	27	E1
Bronti Cl SE17	48	A2
Brook Dr SE11	47	E1
Brook St EC1	31	E3
Brooke Gate W1	37	D1
Brook Grn W6	42	B1
Brooksby St N1	23	E2
Brook's Ms W1	37	F1
Brook St W1	29	F4
Brook St W2	36	B1
Brooksville Av NW6	18	C3
Brookville Rd SW6	43	D4
Broome Way SE5	48	A4
Brougham Rd E8	25	E3
Brown Hart Gdns W1	37	E1
Browning St SE17	48	A2
Brownlow Ms WC1	31	D2
Brownlow Rd E8	25	D3
Brown's Bldgs EC3	32	C4
Brown St W1	29	D4
Broxwood Way NW8	20	C3
Bruckner St W10	27	D1
Brunel Est W2	27	E3
Brune St E1	33	D3
Brunswick Ct SE1	40	C3
Brunswick Gdns W8	35	E2
Brunswick Pl N1	32	B1
Brunswick Pl NW1	29	E2
Brunswick Sq WC1	30	C2
Brushfield St E1	32	C3
Bruton La W1	37	F1
Bruton Pl W1	37	F1
Bruton St W1	37	F1
Bryanston Pl W1	29	D3
Bryanston Sq W1	29	D3
Bryanston St W1	29	D4
Bryant Ct E2	25	D4
Buckfast St E2	33	E1
Buckhurst St E1	33	F2
Buckingham Gate SW1	38	A4
Buckingham Palace Rd SW1	45	F1
Buckingham Rd N1	24	C1
Buckland Cres NW3	20	B2
Buckland St N1	24	B4
Bucklers All SW6	43	D3
Bucklersbury EC4	32	B4
Buckley Rd NW6	19	D2
Bucknall St WC2	30	B4
Buck St NW1	21	F2
Budge's Wk W2	36	A1
Bulinga St SW1	46	B1
Bullace Row SE5	48	B4
Buller Cl SE15	49	E4
Bulmer Pl W11	35	E2
Bulstrode St W1	29	E4
Bulwer St W12	34	A2
Bunhill Row EC1	32	B2
Bunhouse Pl SW1	45	E2
Bunning Way N7	22	C2
Burbage Cl SE1	40	B4
Burder Cl N1	24	C1
Burge St SE1	40	B4
Burgh St N1	23	F4
Burlington Arc W1	38	A1
Burlington Cl W9	27	D2
Burlington Gdns W1	38	A1
Burnaby St SW10	44	A4
Burne Jones Ho W14	43	D1
Burne St NW1	28	C3
Burnham NW3	20	C2
Burnsall St SW3	44	C2
Burnthwaite Rd SW6	43	E4
Burr Cl E1	41	D2
Burrell St SE1	39	F2

54 Bur-Cha

Street	Page	Grid
Burrows Rd NW10	26	A1
Burslem St E1	33	E4
Burton Rd NW6	19	D2
Burton St WC1	30	B1
Burwood Pl W2	28	C4
Bury Pl WC1	30	C3
Bury St EC3	32	C4
Bury St SW1	38	A2
Bury Wk SW3	44	C2
Busby Pl NW5	22	B1
Bush Rd E8	25	F3
Bushwood Dr SE1	49	D1
Bute Gdns W6	42	B1
Bute St SW7	44	B1
Butlers Wf SE1	41	D2
Buttermere Wk E8	25	D1
Butterwick W6	42	A1
Buttesland St N1	32	B1
Buxted Rd E8	25	D2
Buxton St E1	33	D2
Byng Pl WC1	30	B2
Byron Cl E8	25	E3
Byward St EC3	40	C1
Bywater St SW3	45	D2

C

Street	Page	Grid
Cabbell St NW1	28	C3
Cable St E1	41	E1
Cadet Dr SE1	49	E1
Cadiz St SE17	48	A2
Cadogan Gdns SW3	45	D1
Cadogan Gate SW1	45	D1
Cadogan La SW1	37	E4
Cadogan Pl SW1	37	D4
Cadogan Sq SW1	37	D4
Cadogan St SW3	45	D1
Caird St W10	26	C1
Caithness Rd W14	42	B1
Calabria Rd N5	23	F1
Caldwell St SW9	47	D4
Caledonian Rd N1	23	D4
Caledonia St N1	22	C4
Cale St SW3	44	C2
Callcott Rd NW6	19	D2
Callendar Rd SW7	36	B4
Callow St SW3	44	B3
Calshot St N1	23	D4
Calthorpe St WC1	31	D2
Calvert Av E2	32	C1
Calverton SE5	48	C3
Calvin St E1	33	D2
Camberwell New Rd SE5	47	E4
Camberwell Rd SE5	48	A3
Cambria Rd SW6	43	F4
Cambridge Av NW6	19	E4
Cambridge Circ WC2	30	B4
Cambridge Cres E2	25	F4
Cambridge Gdns NW6	19	E4
Cambridge Gdns W10	26	C4
Cambridge Heath Rd E1	25	F4
Cambridge Heath Rd E2	25	F4
Cambridge Pl W8	35	F3
Cambridge Rd NW6	27	E1
Cambridge Sq W2	28	C4
Cambridge St SW1	45	F2
Camden High St NW1	21	F3
Camden Ms NW1	22	B1
Camden Pk Rd NW1	22	B1
Camden Pas N1	23	F3
Camden Rd NW1	22	A3
Camden Sq NW1	22	B1
Camden St NW1	21	F2
Camden Wk N1	23	F3

Street	Page	Grid
Camellia St SW8	46	C4
Camera Pl SW10	44	B3
Camilla Rd SE16	49	F1
Camlet St E2	33	D2
Camley St NW1	22	B2
Camomile St EC3	32	C4
Campden Gro W8	35	E3
Campden Hill Gdns W8	35	E2
Campden Hill Rd W8	35	E2
Campden Hill Sq W8	35	D2
Campden St W8	35	E2
Canal Cl W10	26	B2
Canal Gro SE15	49	E3
Canal Path E2	25	D3
Canal St SE5	48	B3
Canal Wk N1	24	B3
Canal Way W10	26	B2
Canal Way Wk W10	26	B2
Canfield Gdns NW6	20	A2
Canning Pas W8	36	A4
Canning Pl W8	36	A4
Cannon St EC4	32	A4
Cannon St Rd E1	33	F4
Canonbury Cres N1	24	A2
Canonbury Gro N1	24	A2
Canonbury La N1	23	F2
Canonbury Pk N N1	24	A1
Canonbury Pk S N1	24	A1
Canonbury Pl N1	23	F1
Canonbury Rd N1	23	F1
Canonbury Sq N1	23	F2
Canonbury St N1	24	A2
Canonbury Vil N1	23	F2
Canon Row SW1	38	C3
Canon St N1	24	A3
Canrobert St E2	33	F1
Cantelowes Rd NW1	22	B1
Canterbury Pl SE17	47	F1
Canterbury Rd NW6	19	E4
Canterbury Ter NW6	19	E4
Cantium Retail Pk SE1	49	E3
Capland St NW8	28	B2
Capper St WC1	30	A2
Caradoc Cl W2	27	E4
Carburton St W1	29	F3
Cardigan St SE11	47	E2
Cardinal Bourne St SE1	40	B4
Cardine Ms SE15	49	F4
Cardington St NW1	30	A1
Carey St WC2	31	D4
Carlisle La SE1	39	D4
Carlisle Ms NW8	28	B3
Carlisle Pl SW1	38	A4
Carlisle Rd NW6	18	C3
Carlos Pl W1	37	E1
Carlton Gdns SW1	38	B2
Carlton Hill NW8	19	F4
Carlton Ho Ter SW1	38	B2
Carlton Twr Pl SW1	37	D4
Carlton Vale NW6	19	F4
Carlyle Sq SW3	44	B2
Carmelite St EC4	39	E1
Carnaby St W1	30	A4
Carnegie St N1	23	D3
Carnoustie Dr N1	23	D2
Caroline Gdns SE15	49	F4
Caroline Pl W2	35	F1
Caroline Ter SW1	45	E1
Caroline Wk W6	42	C3
Carol St NW1	22	A3
Carriage Dr E SW11	45	E4
Carriage Dr N SW11	45	E3
Carriage Dr W SW11	45	D4
Carroun Rd SW8	47	D4

Street	Page	Grid
Carteret St SW1	38	B3
Carter La EC4	31	F4
Carter Pl SE17	48	A2
Carter St SE17	48	A3
Carting La WC2	38	C1
Cartwright Gdns WC1	30	C1
Cartwright St E1	41	D1
Casey Cl NW8	28	C1
Caspian St SE5	48	B4
Cassidy Rd SW6	43	E4
Casson St E1	33	E3
Castellain Rd W9	27	F2
Casterbridge NW6	19	F3
Castlebrook Cl SE11	47	F1
Castlehaven Rd NW1	21	F2
Castle La SW1	38	A4
Castle Pl NW1	21	F1
Castle Rd NW1	21	F1
Castletown Rd W14	42	C2
Catesby St SE17	48	B1
Cathay St SE16	41	F3
Cathcart Rd SW10	44	A3
Cathcart St NW5	21	F1
Cathedral St SE1	40	B2
Catherine Pl SW1	38	A4
Catherine St WC2	39	D1
Catlin St SE16	49	E2
Cator St SE15	49	D3
Cato St W1	28	C3
Catton St WC1	31	D3
Causton St SW1	46	B1
Cavell St E1	33	F3
Cavendish Av NW8	20	B4
Cavendish Cl NW8	28	B1
Cavendish Pl W1	29	F4
Cavendish Rd NW6	18	C2
Cavendish Sq W1	29	F4
Cavendish St N1	24	B4
Caversham Rd NW5	22	A1
Caversham St SW3	45	D3
Caverswall St W12	26	A4
Caxton Rd W12	34	B3
Caxton St SW1	38	A4
Cedarne Rd SW6	43	F4
Cedar Way NW1	22	B2
Celandine Dr E8	25	D2
Centaur St SE1	39	D4
Central Av SW11	45	D4
Central Mkts EC1	31	F3
Central St EC1	32	A1
Centrepoint WC1	30	B4
Centre St E2	25	F4
Centurion Cl N7	23	D2
Ceylon Rd W14	34	B4
Chadwell St EC1	31	E1
Chadwick St SW1	38	B4
Chagford St NW1	29	D2
Chalbury Wk N1	23	D4
Chalcot Cres NW1	21	D3
Chalcot Gdns NW3	21	D1
Chalcot Rd NW1	21	E2
Chalcot Sq NW1	21	E2
Chaldon Rd SW6	42	C4
Chalk Fm Rd NW1	21	E2
Challoner St W14	43	D2
Chalton St NW1	22	B4
Chamberlayne Rd NW10	26	B1
Chambers St SE16	41	E3
Chamber St E1	41	D1
Chambord St E2	33	D1
Chancellors Rd W6	42	A2
Chancellors St W6	42	A2
Chancel St SE1	39	F2
Chancery La WC2	31	E3

Cha-Coi 55

Name	Page	Grid
Chance St E1	33	D2
Chance St E2	33	D2
Chandler Way SE15	49	D4
Chandos Pl WC2	38	C1
Chandos St W1	29	F3
Chantry St N1	23	F3
Chapel Mkt N1	23	E4
Chapel Pl W1	29	F4
Chapel Side W2	35	F1
Chapel St NW1	28	C3
Chapel St SW1	37	E4
Chaplin Cl SE1	39	E3
Chapman St E1	41	F1
Chapter Rd SE17	47	F2
Chapter St SW1	46	B1
Charecroft Way W12	34	B3
Charing Cross Rd WC2	30	B4
Charlbert St NW8	20	C4
Charles Dickens Ho E2	33	F1
Charles II St SW1	38	B2
Charles Sq N1	32	B1
Charles St W1	37	F2
Charleston St SE17	48	A1
Charleville Rd W14	42	C2
Charlotte Ms W10	26	B4
Charlotte Rd EC2	32	C2
Charlotte St W1	30	A3
Charlotte Ter N1	23	D3
Charlton Pl N1	23	F4
Charlwood Pl SW1	46	A1
Charlwood St SW1	46	A2
Charrington St NW1	22	B4
Charterhouse Sq EC1	31	F3
Charterhouse St EC1	31	F3
Charteris Rd NW6	19	D3
Chart St N1	32	B1
Chatham St SE17	48	B1
Chatsworth Ct W8	43	E1
Chatsworth Rd NW2	18	B1
Chaucer Dr SE1	49	D1
Cheapside EC2	32	A4
Cheesemans Ter W14	43	D2
Chelmsford Rd E18	42	B3
Chelmsford Sq NW10	18	A3
Chelsea Br SW1	45	F3
Chelsea Br SW8	45	F3
Chelsea Br Rd SW1	45	E2
Chelsea Embk SW3	44	C3
Chelsea Manor Gdns SW3	44	C3
Chelsea Manor St SW3	44	C2
Chelsea Pk Gdns SW3	44	B3
Chelsea Sq SW3	44	B2
Chelsea Wf SW10	44	B4
Cheltenham Ter SW3	45	D2
Chenies Pl NW1	22	B4
Chenies St WC1	30	B3
Cheniston Gdns W8	35	F4
Chepstow Cres W11	35	E1
Chepstow Pl W2	27	E4
Chepstow Rd W2	27	E4
Chepstow Vil W11	35	D1
Chepstow Way SE15	49	D4
Cherbury St N1	24	B4
Cherry Gdn St SE16	41	F3
Chesham Ms SW1	37	E4
Chesham Pl SW1	37	E4
Chesham St SW1	37	E4
Cheshire St E2	33	D2
Chesson Rd W14	43	D3
Chester Cl SW1	37	E3
Chester Ct SE5	48	B4
Chesterfield Gdns W1	37	F2
Chesterfield Hill W1	37	F1
Chesterfield St W1	37	F2
Chester Gate NW1	29	F1
Chester Ms SW1	37	F4
Chester Rd NW1	29	E1
Chester Row SW1	45	E1
Chester Sq SW1	37	F4
Chester St E2	33	E2
Chester St SW1	37	E4
Chesterton Rd W10	26	B3
Chester Way SE11	47	E1
Chevening Rd NW6	18	B4
Cheyne Gdns SW3	44	C3
Cheyne Ms SW3	44	C3
Cheyne Pl SW3	45	D3
Cheyne Row SW3	44	C3
Cheyne Wk SW3	44	C3
Cheyne Wk SW10	44	B4
Chicheley St SE1	39	D3
Chichester Rd NW6	19	E4
Chichester Rd W2	27	F3
Chichester St SW1	46	A2
Chicksand St E1	33	D3
Child's Pl SW5	43	E1
Child's St SW5	43	E1
Chiltern St W1	29	E3
Chilton St E2	33	D2
Chilworth Ms W2	28	A4
Chilworth St W2	28	A4
Chippenham Gdns NW6	27	E1
Chippenham Ms W9	27	E2
Chippenham Rd W9	27	E2
Chiswell St EC1	32	A3
Chitty St W1	30	A3
Christchurch Av NW6	18	C2
Christchurch Ct NW6	18	C2
Christchurch St SW3	45	D3
Christian St E1	33	E4
Christopher St EC2	32	B2
Chryssell Rd SW9	47	E4
Chudleigh Rd NW6	18	B2
Chumleigh St SE5	48	C3
Churchill Gdns SW1	46	A2
Churchill Gdns Rd SW1	45	F2
Church Rd N1	24	A1
Church St NW8	28	B3
Church St W2	28	B3
Church St Est NW8	28	B2
Churchway NW1	30	B1
Churton Pl SW1	46	A1
Churton St SW1	46	A1
Cinnabar Wf E1	41	E2
Cinnamon St E1	41	F2
Circus Rd NW8	28	B1
Cirencester St W2	27	F3
City Gdn Row N1	23	F4
City Rd EC1	23	F4
Clabon Ms SW1	37	D4
Clanricarde Gdns W2	35	E1
Claredale St E2	25	E4
Clare La N1	24	A2
Claremont Cl N1	23	E4
Claremont Rd W9	18	C4
Claremont Sq N1	23	E4
Clarence Gdns NW1	29	F1
Clarence Rd NW6	19	D2
Clarence Way NW1	21	F2
Clarence Way Est NW1	21	F2
Clarendon Gdns W9	28	A2
Clarendon Pl W2	36	C1
Clarendon Rd W11	34	C1
Clarendon St SW1	45	F2
Clarendon Wk W11	26	C4
Clare St E2	25	F4
Clareville Gro SW7	44	A1
Clareville St SW7	44	A1
Clarges Ms W1	37	F2
Clarges St W1	37	F2
Clarissa St E8	25	D3
Clarkson Row NW1	22	A4
Clarkson St E2	33	F1
Clark St E1	33	F3
Claverton St SW1	46	A2
Claxton Gro W6	42	B2
Claybrook Rd W6	42	B3
Claylands Pl SW8	47	E4
Claylands Rd SW8	47	D3
Clayton Cres N1	22	C3
Clayton St SE11	47	E3
Clearwell Dr W9	27	F2
Cleaver Sq SE11	47	E2
Cleaver St SE11	47	E2
Clem Attlee Ct SW6	43	D3
Clement Cl NW6	18	A2
Clement's Inn WC2	31	D4
Clements La EC4	40	B1
Clements Rd SE16	41	E4
Clephane Rd N1	24	A1
Clerkenwell Cl EC1	31	E2
Clerkenwell Grn EC1	31	F2
Clerkenwell Rd EC1	31	E3
Cleveland Gdns W2	28	A4
Cleveland Rd N1	24	B2
Cleveland Row SW1	38	A2
Cleveland Sq W2	28	A4
Cleveland St W1	29	F2
Cleveland Ter W2	28	A4
Cleve Rd NW6	19	E2
Clifford Gdns NW10	18	A4
Clifford St W1	38	A1
Cliff Rd NW1	22	B1
Cliff Vil NW1	22	B1
Clifton Cres SE15	49	F4
Clifton Gdns W9	28	A2
Clifton Gro E8	25	E1
Clifton Hill NW8	19	F4
Clifton Pl W2	36	B1
Clifton Rd N1	24	A1
Clifton Rd W9	28	A2
Clifton St EC2	32	C3
Clifton Vil W9	27	F3
Clifton Way SE15	49	F4
Clink St SE1	40	A2
Clipstone Ms W1	30	A2
Clipstone St W1	30	A3
Cliveden Pl SW1	45	E1
Cloak La EC4	40	A1
Clock Twr Pl N7	22	C1
Clonmel Rd SW6	43	D4
Cloth Fair EC1	31	F3
Cloudesley Pl N1	23	E3
Cloudesley Rd N1	23	E3
Cloudesley Sq N1	23	E3
Cloudesley St N1	23	E3
Cloysters Grn E1	41	E2
Club Row E1	33	D2
Club Row E2	33	D2
Cluny Ms SW5	43	E1
Clydesdale Rd W11	27	D4
Coate St E2	25	E4
Cobbett St SW8	47	D4
Cobb St E1	33	D4
Cobourg Rd SE5	49	D3
Cobourg St NW1	30	A1
Cochrane St NW8	20	B4
Cock La EC1	31	F3
Cockspur St SW1	38	B2
Code St E1	33	D3
Coin St SE1	39	E2

56 Coi-Cur

Name	Page	Grid
Coity Rd NW5	21	E1
Coke St E1	33	E4
Colbeck Ms SW7	43	F1
Colebeck Ms N1	23	F1
Colebrooke Row N1	23	F4
Colegrove Rd SE15	49	D4
Coleherne Ct SW5	43	F2
Coleherne Ms SW10	43	F2
Coleherne Rd SW10	43	F2
Coleman Flds N1	24	A3
Coleman Rd SE5	48	C4
Coleman St EC2	32	B4
Coleridge Gdns SW10	43	F4
Coleridge Sq SW10	44	A4
Cole St SE1	40	A3
Colet Gdns W14	42	B1
Coley St WC1	31	D2
College Cres NW3	20	B1
College Cross N1	23	E2
College Pl NW1	22	A3
College Rd NW10	18	A4
Collett Rd SE16	41	E4
Collier St N1	23	D4
Collingham Gdns SW5	43	F1
Collingham Pl SW5	43	F1
Collingham Rd SW5	43	F1
Collingwood St E1	33	F2
Colnbrook St SE1	39	F4
Colombo St SE1	39	F2
Colonnade WC1	30	C2
Colonnades, The W2	27	F4
Colonnade Wk SW1	45	F1
Columbia Rd E2	33	D1
Colville Ct N1	24	C3
Colville Gdns W11	27	D4
Colville Hos W11	27	D4
Colville Rd W11	27	D4
Colville Sq W11	27	D4
Colville Ter W11	27	D4
Colwith Rd W6	42	A3
Colyer Cl N1	23	D4
Comeragh Ms W14	42	C2
Comeragh Rd W14	42	C2
Comfort St SE15	48	C3
Commercial Rd E1	33	E4
Commercial St E1	33	D2
Commercial Way SE15	49	D4
Compayne Gdns NW6	19	F2
Compton Av N1	23	F1
Compton Rd N1	23	F1
Compton Rd NW10	26	B1
Compton St EC1	31	F2
Compton Ter N1	23	F1
Comus Pl SE17	48	C1
Concert Hall App SE1	39	D2
Condray Pl SW11	44	C4
Conduit Ms W2	28	B4
Conduit Pl W2	28	B4
Conduit St W1	37	F1
Coney Wk SW8	47	D3
Congreve St SE17	48	C1
Conistone Way N7	22	C2
Coniston Ho SE5	48	A4
Conlan St W10	26	C2
Connaught Pl W2	37	D1
Connaught Sq W2	29	D4
Connaught St W2	28	C4
Constitution Hill SW1	37	F3
Content St SE17	48	B1
Conway St W1	30	A2
Cooks Rd SE17	47	F3
Coombs St N1	23	F4
Coomer Pl SW6	43	D3
Coopers La NW1	22	B4
Coopers Rd SE1	49	D2
Copenhagen St N1	22	C3
Cope Pl W8	35	E4
Copperfield St SE1	39	F3
Copper Row SE1	41	D2
Copthall Av EC2	32	B4
Copthall Ct EC2	32	B4
Coptic St WC1	30	C3
Coral St SE1	39	E3
Coram St WC1	30	C2
Corbiere Ho N1	24	C3
Corbridge Cres E2	25	F4
Corfield St E2	33	F1
Cork St W1	38	A1
Corlett St NW1	28	C3
Cornelia St N7	23	D1
Cornhill EC3	32	B4
Cornwall Cres W11	34	C1
Cornwall Gdns SW7	35	F4
Cornwall Ms S SW7	36	A4
Cornwall Rd SE1	39	E2
Cornwall Sq SE11	47	F2
Coronet St N1	32	C1
Corporation Row EC1	31	E2
Corsham St N1	32	B1
Corsica St N5	23	F1
Cosser St SE1	39	E4
Cosway St NW1	28	C3
Cotleigh Rd NW6	19	E2
Cottage Grn SE5	48	B4
Cottage Pl SW3	36	C4
Cottesmore Gdns W8	35	F4
Cottingham Rd SW8	47	D4
Coulson St SW3	45	D1
Councillor St SE5	48	A4
County St SE1	40	A4
Courtenay St SE11	47	E2
Courtfield Gdns SW5	43	F1
Courtfield Rd SW7	43	F1
Court Gdns N7	23	C1
Courtnell St W2	27	E4
Courtyard, The N1	23	D2
Covent Gdn WC2	38	C1
Coventry Rd E1	33	F2
Coventry Rd E2	33	F2
Coventry St W1	38	B1
Coverdale Rd NW2	18	B2
Coverley Cl E1	33	E3
Cowcross St EC1	31	F3
Cowdenbeath Path N1	23	D3
Cowper St EC2	32	B2
Crabtree Cl E2	25	D4
Crabtree La SW6	42	B4
Cramond Cl W6	42	C3
Crampton St SE17	47	F1
Cranbourn St WC2	38	B1
Crane Gro N7	23	E1
Cranleigh St NW1	22	A4
Cranley Gdns SW7	44	A2
Cranley Ms SW7	44	A2
Cranley Pl SW7	44	B1
Cranmer Rd SW9	47	C4
Cranston Est N1	24	B4
Cranswick Rd SE16	49	F2
Cranwood St EC1	32	B1
Craven Hill W2	36	A1
Craven Hill Gdns W2	36	A1
Craven Hill Ms W2	36	A1
Craven Pas WC2	38	C2
Craven Rd W2	36	A1
Craven St WC2	38	C2
Craven Ter W2	36	A1
Crawford Pl W1	28	C4
Crawford St W1	29	D3
Creasy Est SE1	40	C4
Crediton Rd NW10	18	B3
Credon Rd SE16	49	F2
Creechurch La EC3	32	C4
Crefeld Cl W6	42	B3
Creighton Rd NW6	18	B4
Cremer St E2	25	D4
Cremorne Rd SW10	44	A4
Crescent Pl SW3	44	C1
Crescent St N1	23	D2
Cresswell Gdns SW5	44	A2
Cresswell Pl SW10	44	A2
Crestfield St WC1	30	C1
Crewdson Rd SW9	47	E4
Cricketers Ct SE11	47	F1
Crimscott St SE1	40	C4
Crinan St N1	22	C4
Cringle St SW8	46	A4
Crispin St E1	33	D3
Crisp Rd W6	42	A2
Crofters Way NW1	22	B3
Crofts St E1	41	E1
Crogsland Rd NW1	21	E2
Cromer St WC1	30	C1
Crompton St W2	28	B2
Cromwell Cres SW5	43	E1
Cromwell Gdns SW7	36	B4
Cromwell Gro W6	34	A4
Cromwell Ms SW7	44	B1
Cromwell Pl SW7	44	B1
Cromwell Rd SW5	43	F1
Cromwell Rd SW7	43	F1
Cromwell Twr EC2	32	A3
Crondall St N1	24	B4
Cronin St SE15	49	D4
Cropley St N1	24	B4
Crosby Row SE1	40	B3
Crossfield Rd NW3	20	B2
Crossley St N7	23	E1
Crossmount Ho SE5	48	A4
Cross St N1	23	F3
Crosswall EC3	41	D1
Croston St E8	25	E3
Crowder St E1	41	F1
Crowland Ter N1	24	B2
Crown Cl NW6	19	F1
Crowndale Rd NW1	22	A4
Crown Pas SW1	38	A2
Crown Pl EC2	32	C3
Crown St SE5	48	A4
Crowthorne Rd W10	26	B4
Croxley Rd W9	27	D1
Crucifix La SE1	40	C3
Cruden St N1	23	F3
Cruikshank St WC1	31	E1
Crutched Friars EC3	40	C1
Cubitt St WC1	31	D1
Cudworth St E1	33	F2
Cuff Pt E2	33	D1
Culford Gdns SW3	45	D1
Culford Gro N1	24	C1
Culford Rd N1	24	C2
Culloden Cl SE16	49	E2
Culmore Rd SE15	49	F4
Culross St W1	37	E1
Cumberland Cl E8	25	D1
Cumberland Cres W14	42	C1
Cumberland Gate W1	37	D1
Cumberland Mkt NW1	29	F1
Cumberland St SW1	45	F2
Cumming St N1	23	D4
Cundy St SW1	45	E1
Cunningham Pl NW8	28	B2
Cureton St SW1	46	B1

Cur-Duk 57

Name	Page	Grid
Curlew St SE1	41	D3
Cursitor St EC4	31	E4
Curtain Rd EC2	32	C2
Curtis St SE1	49	D1
Curtis Way SE1	49	D1
Curzon Gate W1	37	E2
Curzon St W1	37	E2
Custom Ho Wk EC3	40	C1
Cut, The SE1	39	E3
Cuthbert St W2	28	B2
Cutler St E1	32	C4
Cynthia St N1	23	D4
Cyntra Pl E8	25	F2
Cyrus St EC1	31	F2

D

Name	Page	Grid
Dacre St SW1	38	B4
Dagmar Gdns NW10	18	B4
Dagmar Ter N1	23	F3
Dalby St NW5	21	F1
Daleham Ms NW3	20	B1
Dalehead NW1	22	A4
Dale Rd SE17	47	F3
Dalgarno Gdns W10	26	A3
Dalgarno Way W10	26	A2
Dallington St EC1	31	F2
Dalston La E8	25	D1
Dame St N1	24	A4
Damien St E1	33	F4
Danbury St N1	23	F4
Danesfield SE5	48	C3
Daniel Gdns SE15	49	D4
Dante Rd SE11	47	F1
Danvers St SW3	44	B3
D'Arblay St W1	30	A4
Darfield Way W10	26	B4
Darlan Rd SW6	43	D4
Darling Row E1	33	F2
Darnley Rd E9	25	F1
Dartford St SE17	48	A3
Dartmouth Cl W11	27	D4
Dartmouth Rd NW2	18	B1
Dartmouth St SW1	38	B3
Dart St W10	26	C1
Darwin St SE17	48	B1
Date St SE17	48	A2
Davenant St E1	33	E3
Daventry St NW1	28	C3
Davey Cl N7	23	D1
Davey St SE15	49	D3
Davidge St SE1	39	F3
Davidson Gdns SW8	46	C4
Davies St W1	37	F1
Dawes Rd SW6	42	C4
Dawes St SE17	48	B2
Dawlish Rd NW2	18	B1
Dawson Pl W2	35	E1
Dawson St E2	25	D4
Deacon Ms N1	24	B2
Deacon Way SE17	48	A1
Deal St E1	33	E3
Dean Bradley St SW1	38	C4
Deanery St W1	37	E2
Dean Farrar St SW1	38	B4
Dean Rd NW2	18	A1
Dean Ryle St SW1	46	C1
Deans Bldgs SE17	48	B1
Dean Stanley St SW1	38	C4
Dean St W1	30	B4
Dean Trench St SW1	38	C4
De Beauvoir Cres N1	24	C3
De Beauvoir Est N1	24	B3
De Beauvoir Rd N1	24	C3
De Beauvoir Sq N1	24	C2
Decima St SE1	40	C4
Deerhurst Rd NW2	18	B1
Delaford Rd SE16	49	F2
Delaford St SW6	42	C4
Delamere Ter W2	27	F3
Delancey St NW1	21	F3
De Laune St SE17	47	F2
Delaware Rd W9	27	F2
Delhi St N1	22	C3
Dellow St E1	41	F1
Delorme St W6	42	B3
Delverton Rd SE17	47	F2
Denbigh Cl W11	35	D1
Denbigh Pl SW1	46	A2
Denbigh Rd W11	35	D1
Denbigh St SW1	46	A1
Denbigh Ter W11	35	D1
Denholme Rd W9	27	D1
Denmark Gro N1	23	E4
Denmark Rd NW6	19	D4
Denmark St WC2	30	B4
Denne Ter E8	25	D3
Denning Cl NW8	28	A1
Dennington Pk Rd NW6	19	E1
Denny St SE11	47	E2
Denyer St SW3	44	C1
Derbyshire St E2	33	E1
Dericote St E8	25	E3
Dering St W1	29	F4
Derry St W8	35	F3
Desborough Cl W2	27	F3
De Vere Gdns W8	36	A3
Deverell St SE1	40	B4
Devonia Rd N1	23	F4
Devonshire Cl W1	29	F3
Devonshire Gro SE15	49	F3
Devonshire Ms S W1	29	F3
Devonshire Ms W W1	29	F3
Devonshire Pl W1	29	E2
Devonshire St W1	29	F3
Devonshire Ter W2	28	A4
Devon St SE15	49	F3
Dewey Rd N1	23	E4
Dewhurst Rd W14	34	B4
Dial Wk, The W8	35	F3
Diamond St SE15	48	C4
Dibden St N1	23	F3
Dickens Est SE1	41	D3
Dickens Est SE16	41	D3
Dickens Ho NW6	27	E1
Dickens Sq SE1	40	A4
Dighton Ct SE5	48	A3
Dilke St SW3	45	D3
Dingley Pl EC1	32	A1
Dingley Rd EC1	32	A1
Disbrowe Rd W6	42	C3
Discovery Wk E1	41	F2
Diss St E2	33	D1
Distaff La EC4	40	A1
Distillery Rd W6	42	A2
Distin St SE11	47	E1
Dixon Ho W10	26	B4
Dixon's All SE16	41	F3
Dobson Cl NW6	20	B2
Dockhead SE1	41	D3
Dockley Rd SE16	41	E4
Dock St E1	41	E1
Docwra's Bldgs N1	24	C1
Doddington Gro SE17	47	F3
Doddington Pl SE17	47	F3
Dodson St SE1	39	E3
Dolben St SE1	39	F2
Dolland St SE11	47	D2
Dolphin Sq SW1	46	A2
Dombey St WC1	31	D3
Donaldson Rd NW6	19	D3
Donegal St N1	23	D4
Donne Pl SW3	44	C1
Doric Way NW1	30	B1
Dorman Way NW8	20	B3
Dorney NW3	20	C2
Dorrington St EC1	31	E3
Dorset Est E2	33	D1
Dorset Ri EC4	31	F4
Dorset Rd SW8	47	D4
Dorset Sq NW1	29	D2
Dorset St W1	29	E3
Doughty Ms WC1	31	D2
Doughty St WC1	31	D2
Douglas Rd N1	24	A2
Douglas Rd NW6	19	D3
Douglas St SW1	46	B1
Douro Pl W8	35	F4
Dovehouse St SW3	44	B2
Dove Ms SW5	44	A1
Dovercourt Est N1	24	B1
Dove Rd N1	24	B1
Dove Row E2	25	E3
Dover St W1	37	F1
Doves Yd N1	23	E3
Dowgate Hill EC4	40	B1
Dowland St W10	18	C4
Dowlas St SE5	48	C4
Downfield Cl W9	27	F2
Downham Rd N1	24	B2
Downing St SW1	38	C3
Down St W1	37	F2
D'Oyley St SW1	45	E1
Draco St SE17	48	A3
Dragon Rd SE15	48	C3
Drake Ct W12	34	B4
Drakes Ctyd NW6	19	D2
Draycott Av SW3	44	C1
Draycott Pl SW3	45	D1
Draycott Ter SW3	45	D1
Drayford Cl W9	27	D2
Drayson Ms W8	35	E3
Drayton Gdns SW10	44	A2
Dresden Cl NW6	19	F1
Droop St W10	26	C2
Drovers Pl SE15	49	F4
Druid St SE1	40	C3
Drummond Cres NW1	30	B1
Drummond Gate SW1	46	B2
Drummond Rd SE16	41	F4
Drummond St NW1	30	A2
Drury La WC2	30	C4
Dryden Ct SE11	47	E1
Drysdale St N1	32	C1
Dublin Av E8	25	E3
Du Cane Cl W12	26	A4
Duchess of Bedford's Wk W8	35	E3
Duchess St W1	29	F3
Duchy St SE1	39	E2
Dudley Rd NW6	18	C4
Dudley St W2	28	B3
Dufferin St EC1	32	A2
Dugard Way SE11	47	F1
Duke of Wellington Pl SW1	37	E3
Duke of York Sq SW3	45	D1
Duke of York St SW1	38	A2
Dukes La W8	35	E3
Dukes Pl EC3	32	C4
Duke's Rd WC1	30	B1
Duke St SW1	38	A2

58 Duk-Eve

Duke St W1	29	E4
Dulford St W11	34	C1
Dunbridge St E2	33	E2
Duncannon St WC2	38	C1
Duncan Rd E8	25	F3
Duncan St N1	23	F4
Duncan Ter N1	23	F4
Dundee St E1	41	F2
Dundonald Rd NW10	18	B3
Dunloe St E2	25	D4
Dunmore Rd NW6	18	C3
Dunsany Rd W14	34	B4
Dunster Gdns NW6	19	D2
Dunston Rd E8	25	D3
Dunston St E8	25	D3
Dunton Rd SE1	49	D2
Durant St E2	25	E4
Durham St SE11	47	D2
Durham Ter W2	27	F4
Durward St E1	33	F3
Durweston St W1	29	D3
Dyne Rd NW6	19	D2
Dynham Rd NW6	19	E2
Dyott St WC1	30	B4

E

Eagle Ct EC1	31	F3
Eagle St WC1	31	D3
Eagle Wf Rd N1	24	A4
Eamont St NW8	20	C4
Eardley Cres SW5	43	E2
Earlham St WC2	30	B4
Earls Ct Gdns SW5	43	F1
Earls Ct Rd SW5	43	E1
Earls Ct Rd W8	43	E1
Earls Ct Sq SW5	43	F2
Earlsferry Way N1	23	D2
Earlsmead Rd NW10	18	A4
Earls Ter W8	35	D4
Earlston Gro E9	25	F3
Earl St EC2	32	B3
Earls Wk W8	35	E4
Earnshaw St WC2	30	B4
Earsby St W14	42	C1
Eastbourne Ms W2	28	A4
Eastbourne Ter W2	28	A4
Eastcastle St W1	30	A4
Eastcheap EC3	40	B1
East La SE16	41	E3
East Mt St E1	33	F3
East Rd N1	32	B1
East Row W10	26	C2
East Smithfield E1	41	D1
East St SE17	48	A2
East Surrey Gro SE15	49	D4
East Tenter St E1	33	D4
Eaton Cl SW1	45	E1
Eaton Gate SW1	45	E1
Eaton La SW1	37	F4
Eaton Ms N SW1	37	E4
Eaton Ms S SW1	37	F4
Eaton Ms W SW1	45	E1
Eaton Pl SW1	37	E4
Eaton Row SW1	37	F4
Eaton Sq SW1	45	E1
Eaton Ter SW1	45	E1
Ebbisham Dr SW8	47	D3
Ebenezer St N1	32	B1
Ebley Cl SE15	49	D3
Ebor St E1	33	D2
Ebury Br SW1	45	F2
Ebury Br Est SW1	45	F2
Ebury Br Rd SW1	45	E2
Ebury Ms SW1	45	F1
Ebury Sq SW1	45	E1
Ebury St SW1	45	E1
Ecclesbourne Rd N1	24	A2
Eccleston Br SW1	45	F1
Eccleston Ms SW1	37	E4
Eccleston Pl SW1	45	F1
Eccleston Sq SW1	45	F1
Eccleston Sq Ms SW1	45	F1
Eccleston St SW1	37	E4
Eckford St N1	23	E4
Edbrooke Rd W9	27	E2
Edgware Rd W2	28	C4
Edinburgh Gate SW1	37	D3
Edinburgh Ho W9	28	A1
Edis St NW1	21	E3
Edith Gro SW10	44	A3
Edith Rd W14	42	C1
Edith St E2	25	E4
Edith Ter SW10	44	A4
Edith Vil W14	43	D1
Edmund St SE5	48	B4
Edwardes Sq W8	35	E4
Edwards Ms N1	23	E2
Edwards Ms W1	29	E4
Effie Pl SW6	43	E4
Effie Rd SW6	43	E4
Egbert St NW1	21	E3
Egerton Cres SW3	44	C1
Egerton Gdns NW10	18	A3
Egerton Gdns SW3	36	C4
Egerton Gdns Ms SW3	36	C4
Egerton Pl SW3	36	C4
Egerton Ter SW3	36	C4
Elcho St SW11	44	C4
Elcot Av SE15	49	F4
Elder St E1	33	D3
Eldon Rd W8	35	F4
Eldon St EC2	32	B3
Eleanor Rd E8	25	F2
Elephant & Castle SE1	47	F1
Elephant Rd SE17	48	A1
Elgin Av W9	27	F1
Elgin Cres W11	27	D4
Elia Ms N1	23	F4
Elias Pl SW8	47	E3
Elia St N1	23	F4
Elim Est SE1	40	C4
Eliot Ms NW8	20	A4
Elizabeth Av N1	24	A2
Elizabeth Br SW1	45	F1
Elizabeth Est SE17	48	B3
Elizabeth Ms NW3	20	C1
Elizabeth St SW1	45	E1
Elkstone Rd W10	27	D3
Ellaline Rd W6	42	B3
Ellen St E1	33	E4
Ellingfort Rd E8	25	F2
Ellington St N7	23	E1
Elliott Rd SW9	47	F4
Elliott Sq NW3	20	C2
Elliotts Row SE11	47	F1
Ellis St SW1	45	D1
Ellsworth St E2	33	F1
Elmfield Way W9	27	E3
Elm Friars Wk NW1	22	B2
Elmington Est SE5	48	B4
Elmore St N1	24	A2
Elm Pk Gdns SW10	44	B2
Elm Pk La SW3	44	B2
Elm Pk Rd SW3	44	B3
Elm Pl SW7	44	B2
Elm Quay Ct SW8	46	B3
Elms Ms W2	36	B1
Elm St WC1	31	D2
Elm Tree Cl NW8	28	B1
Elm Tree Rd NW8	28	B1
Elrington Rd E8	25	E1
Elsham Rd W14	34	C3
Elsham Ter W14	34	C3
Elsted St SE17	48	B1
Elsworthy Ri NW3	20	C2
Elsworthy Rd NW3	20	C3
Elsworthy Ter NW3	20	C2
Elvaston Ms SW7	36	A4
Elvaston Pl SW7	36	A4
Elverton St SW1	46	B1
Elvis Rd NW2	18	A1
Elwin St E2	33	E1
Elystan Pl SW3	44	C2
Elystan St SW3	44	C1
Embankment Gdns SW3	45	D3
Embankment Pl WC2	38	C2
Emba St SE16	41	E3
Emberton SE5	48	C3
Emerald St WC1	31	D3
Emerson St SE1	40	A2
Emery Hill St SW1	38	A4
Emma St E2	25	F4
Emperor's Gate SW7	35	F4
Empress Pl SW6	43	E2
Empress St SE17	48	A3
Enbrook St W10	26	C1
Endell St WC2	30	C4
Endsleigh Gdns WC1	30	B2
Endsleigh Pl WC1	30	B2
Endsleigh St WC1	30	B2
Enfield Rd N1	24	C2
Enford St W1	29	D3
Englands La NW3	21	D1
Englefield Rd N1	24	B1
Enid St SE16	41	D4
Ennismore Gdns SW7	36	C3
Ennismore Gdns Ms SW7	36	C4
Ennismore Ms SW7	36	C3
Ennismore St SW7	36	C4
Ensign St E1	41	D1
Epirus Ms SW6	43	E4
Epirus Rd SW6	43	D4
Epworth St EC2	32	B2
Erasmus St SW1	46	B1
Eresby Pl NW6	19	E2
Errington Rd W9	27	D2
Errol St EC1	32	A2
Erskine Rd NW3	21	D2
Esmeralda Rd SE1	49	E1
Esmond Rd NW6	19	D3
Essendine Rd W9	27	E2
Essex Rd N1	23	F3
Essex Vil W8	35	E3
Estcourt Rd SW6	43	D4
Esterbrooke St SW1	46	B1
Ethnard Rd SE15	49	F3
Eton Av NW3	20	B2
Eton Coll Rd NW3	21	D1
Eton Rd NW3	21	D2
Eton Vil NW3	21	D1
Eustace Rd SW6	43	E4
Euston Gro NW1	30	B1
Euston Rd N1	30	B2
Euston Rd NW1	29	F2
Euston Sq NW1	30	B1
Euston St NW1	30	A1
Euston Twr NW1	30	A2
Eveline Lowe Est SE16	41	E4
Evelyn Fox Ct W10	26	A3
Evelyn Gdns SW7	44	B2
Evelyn Wk N1	24	B4

Eve-Gib 59

Name	Page	Grid
Evergreen Sq E8	25	D2
Everilda St N1	23	D3
Everington St W6	42	B3
Eversholt St NW1	22	A4
Evesham St W11	34	B1
Ewe Cl N7	22	C1
Ewer St SE1	40	A2
Exchange Sq EC2	32	C3
Exeter St WC2	38	C1
Exhibition Cl W12	34	A1
Exhibition Rd SW7	36	B4
Exmoor St W10	26	B2
Exmouth Mkt EC1	31	E2
Exmouth Pl E8	25	F2
Exon St SE17	48	C2
Exton St SE1	39	E2
Eynham Rd W12	26	A4
Ezra St E2	33	D1

F

Name	Page	Grid
Fabian Rd SW6	43	D4
Fairclough St E1	33	E4
Fairfax Pl NW6	20	A2
Fairfax Pl W14	34	C4
Fairfax Rd NW6	20	A2
Fairhazel Gdns NW6	19	F1
Fairholme Rd W14	42	C2
Fakruddin St E1	33	E2
Falcon Ct EC4	31	E4
Falkirk Ho W9	27	F1
Falkirk St N1	24	C4
Falmouth Rd SE1	40	A4
Fann St EC1	32	A2
Fann St EC2	32	A2
Fanshaw St N1	32	C1
Faraday Rd W10	26	C3
Farmers Rd SE5	47	F4
Farm La SW6	43	E3
Farm St W1	37	F1
Farncombe St SE16	41	E3
Farnham Royal SE11	47	D2
Faroe Rd W14	34	B4
Farrier St NW1	21	F2
Farrier Wk SW10	44	A3
Farringdon La EC1	31	E2
Farringdon Rd EC1	31	E2
Farringdon St EC4	31	F3
Fashion St E1	33	D3
Fassett Rd E8	25	E1
Fassett Sq E8	25	E1
Fawcett St SW10	44	A4
Featherstone St EC1	32	B2
Fellows Ct E2	25	D4
Fellows Rd NW3	20	B2
Felton St N1	24	B3
Fenchurch Av EC3	32	C4
Fenchurch St EC3	40	C1
Fendall St SE1	40	C4
Fenelon Pl W14	43	D1
Fenham Rd SE15	49	E4
Fentiman Rd SW8	46	C3
Ferdinand St NW1	21	E1
Fermoy Rd W9	27	D2
Fernhead Rd W9	27	D2
Fernleigh Cl W9	27	D1
Fernshaw Rd SW10	44	A3
Fetter La EC4	31	E4
Fieldgate St E1	33	E3
Fielding Ho NW6	27	E1
Fielding Rd W14	34	B4
Fielding St SE17	48	A3
Field Rd W6	42	C2
Fields Est E8	25	E2
Field St WC1	31	D1
Fife Ter N1	23	D4
Fifth Av W10	26	C1
Finborough Rd SW10	43	F2
Finchley Pl NW8	20	B4
Finchley Rd NW3	20	A1
Finchley Rd NW8	20	B3
Finch Ms SE15	49	D4
Finnis St E2	33	F1
Finsbury Circ EC2	32	B3
Finsbury Est EC1	31	E1
Finsbury Mkt EC2	32	C2
Finsbury Pavement EC2	32	B3
Finsbury Sq EC2	32	B3
Finsbury St EC2	32	B3
Finstock Rd W10	26	B4
First Av W10	27	D2
First St SW3	44	C1
Fisher St WC1	31	D3
Fisherton St NW8	28	B2
Fish St Hill EC3	40	B1
Fitzalan St SE11	47	D1
Fitzgeorge Av W14	42	C1
Fitzhardinge St W1	29	E4
Fitzjames Av W14	42	C1
Fitzmaurice Pl W1	37	F1
Fitzroy Rd NW1	21	E3
Fitzroy Sq W1	30	A2
Fitzroy St W1	30	A2
Flaxman Ter WC1	30	B1
Fleet St EC4	31	E4
Fleming Rd SE17	47	F3
Fleur de Lis St E1	32	C2
Flinton St SE17	48	C2
Flint St SE17	48	B1
Flood St SW3	44	C2
Flood Wk SW3	44	C3
Floral St WC2	38	C1
Florence St N1	23	F2
Florida St E2	33	E1
Flower Wk, The SW7	36	A3
Foley St W1	30	A3
Folgate St E1	32	C3
Fordham St E1	33	E4
Fordingley Rd W9	27	D1
Ford Sq E1	33	F3
Forest Gro E8	25	D2
Fore St EC2	32	A3
Forest Rd E8	25	D1
Formosa St W9	27	F3
Forset St W1	28	C4
Forsyth Gdns SE17	47	F3
Fort Rd SE1	49	D1
Fortune St EC1	32	A2
Foster La EC2	32	A4
Foubert's Pl W1	30	A4
Foulis Ter SW7	44	B2
Fountain Ms NW3	21	D1
Fountain Sq SW1	45	F1
Fount St SW8	46	B4
Fournier St E1	33	D3
Fourth Av W10	26	C2
Foxcote SE5	48	C2
Foxley Rd SW9	47	E4
Frampton St NW8	28	B2
Francis St SW1	46	A1
Frankland Cl SE16	41	F4
Franklin's Row SW3	45	D2
Frazier St SE1	39	E3
Frean St SE16	41	E4
Frederick Cl W2	36	C1
Frederick Cres SW9	47	F4
Frederick St WC1	31	D1
Freemantle St SE17	48	C2
Frensham St SE15	49	E3
Freshfield Av E8	25	D2
Freston Rd W10	34	B1
Freston Rd W11	34	B1
Friary Est SE15	49	E3
Friary Rd SE15	49	E4
Friday St EC4	32	A4
Friend St EC1	31	F1
Frinstead Ho W10	34	B1
Frith St W1	30	B4
Frithville Gdns W12	34	A2
Frognal Ct NW3	20	A1
Frome St N1	24	A4
Frostic Wk E1	33	D3
Fulford St SE16	41	F3
Fulham Bdy SW6	43	E4
Fulham Palace Rd SW6	42	B4
Fulham Palace Rd W6	42	A2
Fulham Rd SW3	44	A3
Fulham Rd SW6	43	F4
Fulwood Pl WC1	31	D3
Furley Rd SE15	49	E4
Furlong Rd N7	23	E1
Furnival St EC4	31	E4
Fynes St SW1	46	B1

G

Name	Page	Grid
Gabrielle Ct NW3	20	B1
Gainsford St SE1	41	D3
Gaisford St NW5	22	A1
Gales Gdns E2	33	F1
Galleywall Rd SE16	49	F1
Galton St W10	26	C2
Galway St EC1	32	A1
Garden Rd NW8	28	A1
Garden Row SE1	39	F4
Garlick Hill EC4	40	A1
Garlinge Rd NW2	19	D1
Garnies Cl SE15	49	D4
Garrick St WC2	38	C1
Garway Rd W2	27	F4
Gascoigne Pl E2	33	D1
Gascony Av NW6	19	E2
Gaskin St N1	23	F3
Gastein Rd W6	42	B3
Gataker St SE16	41	F4
Gateforth St NW8	28	C2
Gate Ms SW7	36	C3
Gateway SE17	48	A3
Gateways, The SW3	45	D1
Gatliff Rd SW1	45	E2
Gaydon Ho W2	27	F2
Gayfere St SW1	38	C4
Gayhurst Rd E8	25	E2
Gaywood Est SE1	39	F4
Gedling Pl SE1	41	D3
Gee St EC1	32	A2
Geffrye St E2	25	D4
Geldart Rd SE15	49	F4
George Mathers Rd SE11	47	F1
George Row SE16	41	E3
George St W1	29	E4
George Yd W1	37	E1
Georgiana St NW1	22	A3
Geraldine St SE11	39	F4
Gerald Rd SW1	45	E1
Gerrard Rd N1	23	F4
Gerrard St W1	38	B1
Gerridge St SE1	39	E4
Gertrude St SW10	44	A3
Gervase St SE15	49	F4
Gibbs Grn W14	43	D2
Gibraltar Wk E2	33	D1

Street	Page	Grid
Gibson Rd SE11	47	D1
Gibson St N1	23	E3
Gifford St N1	22	C2
Gilbert Rd SE11	47	E1
Gilbert St W1	29	E4
Gilbeys Yd NW1	21	E2
Gillfoot NW1	22	A4
Gilling Ct NW3	20	C1
Gillingham St SW1	45	F1
Gilston Rd SW10	44	A2
Giltspur St EC1	31	F4
Gironde Rd SW6	43	D4
Girton Vil W10	26	B4
Gladstone St SE1	39	F4
Gladys Rd NW6	19	E2
Glasgow Ho W9	19	F4
Glasgow Ter SW1	46	A2
Glasshill St SE1	39	F3
Glasshouse St W1	38	A1
Glasshouse Wk SE11	46	C2
Glazbury Rd W14	42	C1
Glebe Pl SW3	44	C3
Gledhow Gdns SW5	44	A1
Gledstanes Rd W14	42	C2
Glendower Pl SW7	44	B1
Glenfinlas Way SE5	47	F4
Glengall Rd NW6	19	D3
Glengall Rd SE15	49	D3
Glengall Ter SE15	49	D3
Glenilla Rd NW3	20	C1
Glenloch Rd NW3	20	C1
Glenmore Rd NW3	20	C1
Glenroy St W12	26	A4
Glenthorne Rd W6	42	A1
Glentworth St NW1	29	D2
Gliddon Rd W14	42	C1
Globe St SE1	40	A4
Gloucester Av NW1	21	E3
Gloucester Cres NW1	21	F3
Gloucester Gate NW1	21	F4
Gloucester Gro Est SE15	48	C3
Gloucester Ho NW6	19	E4
Gloucester Ms W2	28	A4
Gloucester Pl NW1	29	D2
Gloucester Pl W1	29	D3
Gloucester Rd SW7	36	A4
Gloucester Sq W2	28	B4
Gloucester St SW1	46	A2
Gloucester Ter W2	36	B1
Gloucester Wk W8	35	E3
Gloucester Way EC1	31	E1
Goaters All SW6	43	D4
Godfrey St SW3	44	C2
Goding St SE11	46	C2
Godliman St EC4	32	A4
Godson St N1	23	E4
Golborne Rd W10	26	C3
Golden Jubilee Br SE1	38	C2
Golden Jubilee Br WC2	38	C2
Golden La EC1	32	A2
Golden Sq W1	38	A1
Goldhurst Ter NW6	19	F2
Golding St E1	33	E4
Goldington Cres NW1	22	B4
Goldington St NW1	22	B4
Goldman Cl E2	33	E2
Goldney Rd W9	27	E2
Goldsmith's Row E2	25	E4
Goldsmith's Sq E2	25	E4
Goodge St W1	30	A3
Goodinge Cl N7	22	C1
Goodman's Stile E1	33	E4
Goodmans Yd E1	41	D1
Goods Way NW1	22	C4
Goodwin Cl SE16	41	E4
Gopsall St N1	24	B3
Gordon Ct W12	26	A4
Gordon Pl W8	35	E3
Gordon Sq WC1	30	B2
Gordon St WC1	30	B2
Gorefield Pl NW6	19	E4
Gore St SW7	36	A4
Goring St EC3	32	C4
Gorleston St W14	42	C1
Gorsuch St E2	33	D1
Gosfield St W1	30	A3
Gosset St E2	33	D1
Goswell Rd EC1	31	F1
Gough Sq EC4	31	E4
Gough St WC1	31	D2
Goulston St E1	33	D4
Gower Ms WC1	30	B3
Gower Pl WC1	30	A2
Gower St WC1	30	A2
Gower's Wk E1	33	E4
Gracechurch St EC3	40	B1
Grace's All E1	41	E1
Grafton Cres NW1	21	F1
Grafton Pl NW1	30	B1
Grafton St W1	37	F1
Grafton Way W1	30	A2
Grafton Way WC1	30	A2
Graham Rd E8	25	D1
Graham St N1	23	F4
Graham Ter SW1	45	E1
Granary Rd E1	33	F2
Granary St NW1	22	B3
Granby St E2	33	D2
Granby Ter NW1	22	A4
Grand Junct Wf N1	24	A4
Grand Union Cres E8	25	E2
Grand Union Wk NW1	21	F2
Grange, The SE1	41	D4
Grange Gro N1	23	F1
Grange Pl NW6	19	E2
Grange Rd SE1	40	C4
Grange St N1	24	B3
Grange Yd SE1	41	D4
Gransden Av E8	25	F2
Grantbridge St N1	23	F4
Grantully Rd W9	27	F1
Granville Ct N1	24	B3
Granville Pl W1	29	E4
Granville Rd NW6	19	E4
Granville Sq SE15	48	C4
Granville Sq WC1	31	D1
Gratton Rd W14	34	C4
Grayling Sq E2	33	E1
Gray's Inn WC1	31	E3
Gray's Inn Rd WC1	31	D1
Great Castle St W1	30	A4
Great Cen St NW1	29	D3
Great Chapel St W1	30	B4
Great Ch La W6	42	B2
Great Coll St SW1	38	C4
Great Cumberland Pl W1	29	D4
Great Dover St SE1	40	A3
Great Eastern St EC2	32	C1
Great George St SW1	38	B3
Great Guildford St SE1	40	A2
Great James St WC1	31	D3
Great Marlborough St W1	30	A4
Great Maze Pond SE1	40	B3
Greatorex St E1	33	E3
Great Ormond St WC1	30	C3
Great Percy St WC1	31	D1
Great Peter St SW1	38	B4
Great Portland St W1	29	F2
Great Pulteney St W1	38	A1
Great Queen St WC2	30	C4
Great Russell St WC1	30	C3
Great St. Helens EC3	32	C4
Great Scotland Yd SW1	38	C2
Great Smith St SW1	38	B4
Great Suffolk St SE1	39	F2
Great Sutton St EC1	31	F2
Great Titchfield St W1	30	A4
Great Twr St EC3	40	C1
Great Western Rd W2	27	D3
Great Western Rd W9	27	D3
Great Western Rd W11	27	D3
Great Winchester St EC2	32	B4
Great Windmill St W1	38	B1
Greek St W1	30	B4
Green Bk E1	41	F2
Greenberry St NW8	20	C4
Greencoat Pl SW1	46	A1
Greencroft Gdns NW6	19	F2
Greenfield Rd E1	33	E3
Greenham Cl SE1	39	E3
Green Hundred Rd SE15	49	E3
Greenland Rd NW1	22	A3
Greenman St N1	24	A2
Green St W1	37	E1
Greenwell St W1	29	F2
Greenwood Ct SW1	46	A2
Greenwood Rd E8	25	E1
Greet St SE1	39	E2
Gregory Pl W8	35	F3
Grendon St NW8	28	C2
Grenfell Rd W11	34	B1
Grenfell Twr W11	34	B1
Grenfell Wk W11	34	B1
Grenville Ms SW7	44	A1
Grenville Pl SW7	36	A4
Grenville St WC1	30	C2
Gresham St EC2	32	A4
Gresse St W1	30	B3
Greville Hall NW6	19	F4
Greville Pl NW6	19	F4
Greville Rd NW6	19	F3
Greville St EC1	31	E3
Greycoat Pl SW1	38	B4
Greycoat St SW1	38	B4
Grey Eagle St E1	33	D3
Greyhound Rd W6	42	B3
Greyhound Rd W14	42	C3
Grittleton Rd W9	27	E2
Groom Pl SW1	37	E4
Grosvenor Ct NW6	18	B3
Grosvenor Cres SW1	37	E3
Grosvenor Cres Ms SW1	37	E3
Grosvenor Est SW1	46	B1
Grosvenor Gdns SW1	37	F4
Grosvenor Gate W1	37	D1
Grosvenor Hill W1	37	F1
Grosvenor Pk SE5	48	A3
Grosvenor Pl SW1	37	E3
Grosvenor Rd SW1	45	F3
Grosvenor Sq W1	37	E1
Grosvenor St W1	37	F1
Grosvenor Ter SE5	47	F4
Grove Cotts SW3	44	C3
Grove End Rd NW8	28	B1
Grove Ms W6	34	A4
Grove Pas E2	25	F4
Grove Rd NW2	18	A1
Guildhouse St SW1	46	A1
Guilford Pl WC1	31	D2
Guilford St WC1	30	C2

Gui-Hin

Name	Page	Grid
Guinness Trust Bldgs SE11	47	F2
Gun St E1	33	D3
Gunter Gro SW10	44	A3
Gunterstone Rd W14	42	C1
Gunthorpe St E1	33	D3
Gutter La EC2	32	A4
Guy St SE1	40	B3
Gwendwr Rd W14	42	C2
Gwyn Cl SW6	44	A4

H

Name	Page	Grid
Haarlem Rd W14	34	B4
Haberdasher St N1	32	B1
Hackney Rd E2	33	D1
Hadley St NW1	21	F1
Hadrian Est E2	25	E4
Haggerston Rd E8	25	D2
Hainton Cl E1	33	F4
Halcomb St N1	24	C3
Haldane Rd SW6	43	D4
Half Moon Cres N1	23	D4
Half Moon St W1	37	F2
Halford Rd SW6	43	E3
Halkin Arc SW1	37	D4
Halkin Pl SW1	37	E4
Halkin St SW1	37	E3
Hallam St W1	29	F3
Hallfield Est W2	28	A4
Halliford St N1	24	A2
Hall Pl W2	28	B2
Hall Rd NW8	28	A1
Hall St EC1	31	F1
Hall Twr W2	28	B3
Halsey St SW3	45	D1
Halstow Rd NW10	26	B3
Halton Cross St N1	23	F3
Halton Rd N1	23	F2
Hamilton Cl NW8	28	B1
Hamilton Gdns NW8	28	A1
Hamilton Pl W1	37	E2
Hamilton Ter NW8	19	F4
Hammersmith Br Rd W6	42	A2
Hammersmith Bdy W6	42	A1
Hammersmith Flyover W6	42	A2
Hammersmith Gro W6	34	A4
Hammersmith Rd W6	42	B1
Hammersmith Rd W14	42	B1
Hammond St NW5	22	A1
Hampstead Rd NW1	22	A4
Hampton Cl NW6	27	E1
Hampton St SE1	47	F1
Hampton St SE17	47	F1
Hanbury St E1	33	D3
Hand Ct WC1	31	D3
Handel St WC1	30	C2
Handforth Rd SW9	47	E4
Hankey Pl SE1	40	B3
Hannell Rd SW6	42	C4
Hanover Gdns SE11	47	E3
Hanover Gate NW1	28	C1
Hanover Rd NW10	18	A2
Hanover Sq W1	29	F4
Hanover St W1	29	F4
Hanover Ter NW1	28	C1
Hans Cres SW1	37	D4
Hanson St W1	30	A3
Hans Pl SW1	37	D4
Hans Rd SW3	37	D4
Hanway St W1	30	B4
Harben Rd NW6	20	A2
Harbet Rd W2	28	B3
Harcourt St W1	28	C3
Harcourt Ter SW10	43	F2
Hardwick St EC1	31	E1
Harecourt Rd N1	24	A1
Hare Row E2	25	F4
Hare Wk N1	24	C4
Harewood Av NW1	28	C2
Harleyford Rd SE11	47	D3
Harleyford St SE11	47	E3
Harley Gdns SW10	44	A2
Harley Pl W1	29	F3
Harley Rd NW3	20	B2
Harley St W1	29	F2
Harmood St NW1	21	F2
Harmsworth St SE17	47	F2
Harold St SE1	40	C4
Harold Pl SE11	47	E2
Harper Rd SE1	40	A4
Harpur St WC1	31	D3
Harriet Cl E8	25	E3
Harriet Wk SW1	37	D3
Harrington Gdns SW7	43	F1
Harrington Rd SW7	44	B1
Harrington Sq NW1	22	A4
Harrington St NW1	30	A1
Harrison St WC1	30	C1
Harris St SE5	48	B4
Harrowby St W1	28	C4
Harrow Pl E1	32	C4
Harrow Rd W2	27	D2
Harrow Rd W9	27	D2
Harrow Rd W10	26	B2
Hartismere Rd SW6	43	D4
Hartland Rd NW1	21	F2
Hartland Rd NW6	19	D4
Harvey St N1	24	B3
Harvist Rd NW6	26	B1
Harwood Rd SW6	43	E4
Hasker St SW3	44	C1
Haslam Cl N1	23	E2
Haslam St SE15	49	D4
Hastings Cl SE15	49	E4
Hastings St WC1	30	C1
Hatfields SE1	39	F2
Hatherley Gro W2	27	F4
Hatton Gdn EC1	31	E3
Hatton Pl EC1	31	E2
Hatton Wall EC1	31	E3
Haul Rd NW1	22	C4
Havelock St N1	22	C3
Havelock Ter SW8	45	F4
Haverstock St N1	23	F4
Havil St SE5	48	C4
Hawes St N1	23	F2
Hawksmoor St W6	42	B3
Hawley Cres NW1	21	F2
Hawley Rd NW1	21	F2
Hawley St NW1	21	F2
Hawthorne Cl N1	24	C1
Hawtrey Rd NW3	20	C2
Hay Hill W1	37	F1
Hayles St SE11	47	F1
Haymarket SW1	38	B1
Haymerle Rd SE15	49	E3
Hay's Galleria SE1	40	C2
Hay's Ms W1	37	F1
Hay St E2	25	E3
Hazelmere Rd NW6	19	E3
Hazel Rd NW10	26	A1
Hazlewood Cres W10	26	C2
Hazlitt Rd W14	34	C4
Headfort Pl SW1	37	E3
Headlam St E1	33	F2
Healey St NW1	21	F1
Hearn St EC2	32	C2
Heathcote St WC1	31	D2
Heathfield Pk NW2	18	A1
Heddon St W1	38	A1
Heiron St SE17	47	F3
Helmet Row EC1	32	A2
Helmsley Pl E8	25	F2
Hemans St SW8	46	B4
Hemingford Rd N1	23	D3
Hemming St E1	33	E2
Hemp Wk SE17	48	B1
Hemstal Rd NW6	19	E2
Hemsworth St N1	24	C4
Heneage St E1	33	D2
Henley Dr SE1	49	D1
Henley Rd NW10	18	A3
Henrietta Pl W1	29	F4
Henrietta St WC2	38	C1
Henriques St E1	33	E4
Henry Dickens Ct W11	34	B2
Henshall St N1	24	B1
Henshaw St SE17	48	B1
Henstridge Pl NW8	20	C4
Henty Cl SW11	44	C4
Herbal Hill EC1	31	E2
Herbert St NW5	21	E1
Herbrand St WC1	30	C2
Hercules Rd SE1	39	D4
Hereford Ho NW6	19	E4
Hereford Rd W2	27	E4
Hereford Sq SW7	44	A1
Hereford St E2	33	E2
Hermitage St W2	28	B3
Hermitage Wall E1	41	E2
Hermit St EC1	31	F1
Herrick St SW1	46	B1
Herries St W10	18	C4
Hertford Rd N1	24	C3
Hertford St W1	37	F2
Hesketh Pl W11	34	C1
Hesper Ms SW5	43	F2
Hessel St E1	33	F4
Hester Rd SW11	44	C4
Hewer St W10	26	B3
Heyford Av SW8	46	C4
Heygate St SE17	48	A1
Hide Pl SW1	46	B1
Hide Twr SW1	46	B1
Highbury Cor N5	23	E1
Highbury Gro N5	23	F1
Highbury Pl N5	23	F1
Highbury Sta Rd N1	23	E1
High Holborn WC1	30	C4
Highlever Rd W10	26	A3
High Timber St EC4	40	A1
Highway, The E1	41	F1
Highway, The E14	41	F1
Hilary Cl SW6	43	F4
Hildyard Rd SW6	43	E3
Hiley Rd NW10	26	B1
Hilgrove Rd NW6	20	A2
Hill Fm Rd W10	26	A3
Hillgate Pl W8	35	E2
Hillgate St W8	35	E2
Hillingdon St SE5	47	F4
Hillingdon St SE17	47	F4
Hillman Dr W10	26	A2
Hillman St E8	25	F1
Hill Rd NW8	20	A4
Hillside Cl NW8	19	F4
Hillsleigh Rd W8	35	D2
Hill St W1	37	F2
Hilltop Rd NW6	19	E2
Hinde St W1	29	E4

Name	Page	Grid
Hippodrome Pl W11	34	C1
Hobart Pl SW1	37	F4
Hobury St SW10	44	A3
Hofland Rd W14	34	B4
Hogarth Rd SW5	43	F1
Holbeck Row SE15	49	E4
Holbein Ms SW1	45	E2
Holbein Pl SW1	45	E1
Holborn EC1	31	E3
Holborn Viaduct EC1	31	E3
Holford St WC1	31	E1
Holland Gdns W14	34	C4
Holland Gro SW9	47	E4
Holland Pk W8	35	D3
Holland Pk W11	34	C3
Holland Pk Av W11	34	C3
Holland Pk Gdns W14	34	C2
Holland Pk Ms W11	34	C2
Holland Pk Rd W14	35	D4
Holland Pk Roundabout W11	34	B3
Holland Rd W14	34	B3
Holland St SE1	39	F2
Holland St W8	35	E3
Holland Vil Rd W14	34	C3
Holland Wk W8	35	D3
Hollen St W1	30	A4
Holles St W1	29	F4
Hollybush Gdns E2	33	F1
Holly St E8	25	D1
Hollywood Rd SW10	44	A3
Holmead Rd SW6	43	F4
Holmefield Ct NW3	20	C1
Holmes Ter SE1	39	E3
Holms St E2	25	E4
Holyport Rd SW6	42	A4
Holywell La EC2	32	C2
Holywell Row EC2	32	C2
Homefield St N1	24	C4
Homer Row W1	28	C3
Homer St W1	28	C3
Homestead Rd SW6	43	D4
Honeyman Cl NW6	18	B2
Honiton Rd NW6	19	D4
Hooper St E1	33	E4
Hopefield Av NW6	18	C4
Hopewell St SE5	48	B4
Hopton Gdns SE1	39	F2
Hopton St SE1	39	F2
Hopwood Rd SE17	48	B3
Horatio St E2	25	D4
Horbury Cres W11	35	E1
Hormead Rd W9	27	D2
Hornby Cl NW3	20	B2
Hornton Pl W8	35	E3
Hornton St W8	35	E2
Horseferry Rd SW1	46	B1
Horse Guards Av SW1	38	C2
Horse Guards Rd SW1	38	B2
Horselydown La SE1	41	D3
Horse Ride SW1	38	A2
Horsley St SE17	48	B3
Hortensia Rd SW10	44	A4
Horton Rd E8	25	F1
Hosier La EC1	31	F3
Hotspur St SE11	47	E2
Houndsditch EC3	32	C4
Howick Pl SW1	38	A4
Howie St SW11	44	C4
Howitt Rd NW3	20	C1
Howland St W1	30	A3
Howley Pl W2	28	A3
Hows St E2	25	D4
Hoxton Sq N1	32	C1
Hoxton St N1	24	C3
Hugh Dalton Av SW6	43	D3
Hugh Gaitskell Cl SW6	43	D3
Hugh St SW1	45	F1
Huguenot Pl E1	33	D3
Humber Dr W10	26	B2
Humbolt Rd W6	42	C3
Humphrey St SE1	49	D2
Hungerford Br SE1	38	C2
Hungerford Br WC2	38	C2
Hunt Cl W11	34	B2
Hunter St WC1	30	C2
Huntingdon St N1	23	D2
Huntley St WC1	30	A2
Hunton St E1	33	E2
Huntsman St SE17	48	B1
Hurstway Wk W11	34	B1
Huson Cl NW3	20	C2
Huxley St W10	26	C1
Hyde Pk SW7	36	C2
Hyde Pk W1	36	C2
Hyde Pk W2	36	C2
Hyde Pk Cor W1	37	E3
Hyde Pk Cres W2	28	C4
Hyde Pk Gdns W2	36	B1
Hyde Pk Gate SW7	36	A3
Hyde Pk Pl W2	36	C1
Hyde Pk Sq W2	28	C4
Hyde Pk St W2	28	C4
Hyde Rd N1	24	B3
Hyndman St SE15	49	F3

I

Name	Page	Grid
Ifield Rd SW10	43	F3
Ilbert St W10	26	B1
Ilchester Gdns W2	35	F1
Ilchester Pl W14	35	D4
Ilderton Rd SE16	49	F2
Iliffe St SE17	47	F2
Imber St N1	24	B3
Imperial Coll Rd SW7	36	B4
Inkerman Rd NW5	21	F1
Inner Circle NW1	29	E1
Inverness Pl W2	35	F1
Inverness St NW1	21	F3
Inverness Ter W2	35	F1
Inville Rd SE17	48	B2
Ireland Yd EC4	31	F4
Ironmonger Row EC1	32	A1
Irving Rd W14	34	B4
Irving St WC2	38	B1
Isabella St SE1	39	F2
Islington Grn N1	23	F3
Islington High St N1	23	F4
Islington Pk St N1	23	E2
Ivatt Pl W14	43	D2
Iverna Ct W8	35	E4
Iverna Gdns W8	35	E4
Iverson Rd NW6	19	D1
Ives St SW3	44	C1
Ivimey St E2	33	E1
Ivor Pl NW1	29	D2
Ivor St NW1	22	A2
Ivy St N1	24	C4
Ixworth Pl SW3	44	C2

J

Name	Page	Grid
Jacaranda Gro E8	25	D2
Jackman St E8	25	F3
Jacob St SE1	41	D3
Jago Wk SE5	48	B4
Jamaica Rd SE1	41	D3
Jamaica Rd SE16	41	D3
Jameson St W8	35	E2
James St W1	29	E4
Jamestown Rd NW1	21	F3
Janeway St SE16	41	E3
Jay Ms SW7	36	A3
Jeffreys St NW1	21	F2
Jeger Av E2	25	D3
Jerdan Pl SW6	43	E4
Jermyn St SW1	38	B1
Jerome Cres NW8	28	C2
Jewry St EC3	33	D4
Joan St SE1	39	F2
Jockey's Flds WC1	31	D3
John Adam St WC2	38	C1
John Aird Ct W2	28	A3
John Carpenter St EC4	39	F1
John Felton Rd SE16	41	E3
John Fisher St E1	41	E1
John Islip St SW1	46	C1
John Maurice Cl SE17	48	B1
John Princes St W1	29	F4
John Roll Way SE16	41	E4
John Ruskin St SE5	47	F4
John's Ms WC1	31	D2
John Smith Av SW6	43	D4
Johnson Cl E8	25	E3
Johnson's Pl SW1	46	A2
John Spencer Sq N1	23	F1
John St WC1	31	D2
Jonathan St SE11	47	D2
Jowett St SE15	49	D4
Jubilee Pl SW3	44	C2
Judd St WC1	30	C1
Juer St SW11	44	C4
Juniper Cres NW1	21	E2
Jupiter Way N7	23	D1
Juxon St SE11	47	D1

K

Name	Page	Grid
Kay St E2	25	E4
Kean St WC2	31	D4
Keeley St WC2	31	D4
Keetons Rd SE16	41	E4
Kelfield Gdns W10	26	A4
Kelly Av SE15	49	D4
Kelly St NW1	21	F1
Kelsey St E2	33	F2
Kelso Pl W8	35	F4
Kelvedon Rd SW6	43	D4
Kemble St WC2	31	D4
Kempe Rd NW6	18	B4
Kempsford Gdns SW5	43	E2
Kempsford Rd SE11	47	E1
Kenchester Cl SW8	46	C4
Kendal Cl SW9	47	F4
Kendal St W2	28	C4
Kendrick Pl SW7	44	B1
Kenilworth Rd NW6	19	D3
Kenley Wk W11	34	C1
Kennet Rd W9	27	D2
Kennet St E1	41	E1
Kennings Way SE11	47	E2
Kenning Ter N1	24	C3
Kennington La SE11	47	D2
Kennington Oval SE11	47	D3
Kennington Pk SW9	47	E4
Kennington Pk Gdns SE11	47	F3
Kennington Pk Pl SE11	47	E3
Kennington Pk Rd SE11	47	E3
Kennington Rd SE1	39	D4
Kennington Rd SE11	47	E1

Ken-Lei 63

Name	Page	Grid
Kensal Rd W10	26	C2
Kensington Ch Ct W8	35	F3
Kensington Ch St W8	35	E2
Kensington Ch Wk W8	35	F3
Kensington Ct W8	35	F3
Kensington Ct Pl W8	35	F4
Kensington Gdns W2	36	A2
Kensington Gdns Sq W2	27	F4
Kensington Gate W8	36	A4
Kensington Gore SW7	36	B3
Kensington High St W8	35	E4
Kensington High St W14	42	C1
Kensington Mall W8	35	E2
Kensington Palace Gdns W8	35	F2
Kensington Pk Gdns W11	35	D1
Kensington Pk Rd W11	35	D1
Kensington Pl W8	35	E2
Kensington Rd SW7	36	B3
Kensington Rd W8	35	F3
Kensington Sq W8	35	F3
Kentish Town Rd NW1	21	F2
Kentish Town Rd NW5	21	F2
Kenton St WC1	30	C2
Kent Pas NW1	29	D1
Kent St E2	25	D4
Kent Ter NW1	28	C1
Kenway Rd SW5	43	F1
Keppel St WC1	30	B3
Kerridge Ct N1	24	C1
Keslake Rd NW6	18	B4
Kestrel Ho EC1	31	F1
Kevan Ho SE5	48	A4
Keybridge Ho SW8	46	C3
Key Cl E1	33	F2
Keyworth St SE1	39	F4
Kibworth St SW8	47	D4
Kilburn High Rd NW6	19	D2
Kilburn La W9	26	B1
Kilburn La W10	26	B1
Kilburn Pk Rd NW6	27	E1
Kilburn Pl NW6	19	E3
Kilburn Priory NW6	19	F3
Kilburn Sq NW6	19	E3
Kildare Gdns W2	27	E4
Kildare Ter W2	27	E4
Killick St N1	23	D4
Kilmaine Rd SW6	42	C4
Kilmarsh Rd W6	42	A1
Kilravock St W10	26	C1
Kimberley Rd NW6	18	C3
Kincaid Rd SE15	49	F4
King & Queen St SE17	48	A2
King Charles St SW1	38	B3
Kingdon Rd NW6	19	E1
King Edwards Rd E9	25	F3
King Edward St EC1	32	A4
King Edward Wk SE1	39	E4
Kingham Cl W11	34	C3
King Henry's Reach W6	42	A3
King Henry's Rd NW3	20	C2
King Henry's Wk N1	24	C1
King James St SE1	39	F3
Kinglake St SE17	48	C2
Kingly St W1	30	A4
Kingsbridge Rd W10	26	A4
Kingsbury Rd N1	24	C1
Kingsbury Ter N1	24	C1
Kings Coll Rd NW3	20	C2
Kingscroft Rd NW2	19	D1
King's Cross Rd WC1	31	D1
Kingsdale Gdns W11	34	B2
Kingsdown Cl W10	26	B4
Kingsgate Pl NW6	19	E2
Kingsgate Rd NW6	19	E2
Kings Gro SE15	49	F4
Kingsland Grn E8	24	C1
Kingsland Rd E2	24	C4
Kingsland Rd E8	24	C4
Kingsland Shop Cen E8	25	D1
Kingsley Rd NW6	19	D3
Kings Mall W6	42	A1
King's Ms WC1	31	D3
Kingsmill Ter NW8	20	B4
King's Reach Twr SE1	39	E2
King's Rd SW1	45	D2
King's Rd SW3	45	D2
Kingstown St NW1	21	E3
King St EC2	32	A4
King St SW1	38	A2
King St WC2	38	C1
Kingsway WC2	31	D4
Kingswood Av NW6	18	C3
Kingswood Cl SW8	46	C4
King William St EC4	40	B1
Kinnerton St SW1	37	E3
Kinnoul Rd W6	42	C3
Kipling Est SE1	40	B3
Kipling St SE1	40	B3
Kirby Est SE16	41	F4
Kirby Gro SE1	40	C3
Kirkland Wk E8	25	D1
Kirtling St SW8	46	A4
Kirwyn Way SE5	47	F4
Kitson Rd SE5	48	B4
Knaresborough Pl SW5	43	F1
Knighten St E1	41	E2
Knightsbridge SW1	37	D3
Knightsbridge SW7	36	C3
Knivet Rd SW6	43	E3
Knox St W1	29	D3
Kylemore Rd NW6	19	E2
Kynance Ms SW7	35	F4
Kynance Pl SW7	36	A4

L

Name	Page	Grid
Laburnum St E2	25	D3
Lackington St EC2	32	B3
Ladbroke Gdns W11	35	D1
Ladbroke Gro W10	26	B2
Ladbroke Gro W11	26	C4
Ladbroke Rd W11	35	D2
Ladbroke Sq W11	35	D1
Ladbroke Ter W11	35	D1
Ladbroke Wk W11	35	D2
Lafone St SE1	41	D3
Laird Ho SE5	48	A4
Lakeside Rd W14	34	B4
Lambert St N1	23	E2
Lambeth Br SE1	46	C1
Lambeth Br SW1	46	C1
Lambeth High St SE1	47	D1
Lambeth Hill EC4	40	A1
Lambeth Palace Rd SE1	39	D4
Lambeth Rd SE1	47	D1
Lambeth Rd SE11	47	D1
Lambeth Wk SE11	47	D1
Lamb La E8	25	F2
Lambolle Pl NW3	20	C1
Lambolle Rd NW3	20	C1
Lamb's Conduit St WC1	31	D2
Lamb's Pas EC1	32	B3
Lamb St E1	33	D3
Lamont Rd SW10	44	A3
Lanark Pl W9	28	A2
Lanark Rd W9	19	F4
Lancaster Ct SW6	43	D4
Lancaster Dr NW3	20	C1
Lancaster Gate W2	36	A1
Lancaster Gro NW3	20	B1
Lancaster Ms W2	36	A1
Lancaster Pl WC2	39	D1
Lancaster Rd W11	26	C4
Lancaster St SE1	39	F3
Lancaster Ter W2	36	B1
Lancaster Wk W2	36	A2
Lancefield St W10	27	D1
Lancelot Pl SW7	37	D3
Lancresse Ct N1	24	C3
Landon Pl SW1	37	D4
Langdale Cl SE17	48	A3
Langford Ct NW8	20	A4
Langford Pl NW8	20	A4
Langham Pl W1	29	F3
Langham St W1	29	F3
Langler Rd NW10	18	A4
Langley La SW8	47	D3
Langley St WC2	30	C4
Langthorne St SW6	42	B4
Langton Rd SW9	47	F4
Langton St SW10	44	A3
Langtry Rd NW8	19	F3
Lanhill Rd W9	27	E2
Lansdowne Cres W11	34	C1
Lansdowne Dr E8	25	E1
Lansdowne Ri W11	34	C1
Lansdowne Rd W11	34	C1
Lansdowne Ter WC1	30	C2
Lansdowne Wk W11	34	C2
Lant St SE1	40	A3
Lapford Cl W9	27	D2
Larcom St SE17	48	A1
Larnach Rd W6	42	B3
Latimer Pl W10	26	A4
Latimer Rd W10	26	A4
Latona Rd SE15	49	E3
Latymer Ct W6	42	B1
Lauderdale Rd W9	27	F1
Lauderdale Twr EC2	32	A3
Launceston Pl W8	36	A4
Laundry Rd W6	42	C3
Laurel St E8	25	D1
Lavender Gro E8	25	D2
Laverton Pl SW5	43	F1
Lavington St SE1	39	F2
Lawford Rd N1	24	C2
Lawford Rd NW5	22	A1
Lawn La SW8	46	C3
Lawrence St SW3	44	C3
Lawson Est SE1	40	B4
Law St SE1	40	B4
Laxley Cl SE5	47	F4
Layard Rd SE16	49	F1
Layard Sq SE16	49	F1
Laycock St N1	23	E1
Laystall St EC1	31	E2
Leadenhall St EC3	32	C4
Leake St SE1	39	D3
Leamington Rd Vil W11	27	D3
Leather La EC1	31	E3
Leathermarket Ct SE1	40	C3
Leathermarket St SE1	40	C3
Lecky St SW7	44	B2
Ledbury Est SE15	49	F4
Ledbury Rd W11	27	D4
Ledbury St SE15	49	E4
Leeke St WC1	31	D1
Lees Pl W1	37	E1
Lee St E8	25	D3
Legion Cl N1	23	E1
Leicester Sq WC2	38	B1

Name	Page	Grid
Leigh Gdns NW10	18	A4
Leigh St WC1	30	C2
Leinster Gdns W2	28	A4
Leinster Ms W2	36	A1
Leinster Pl W2	28	A4
Leinster Sq W2	27	E4
Leinster Ter W2	36	A1
Leman St E1	33	D4
Lena Gdns W6	34	A4
Lennox Gdns SW1	37	D4
Lennox Gdns Ms SW1	37	D4
Lenthall Rd E8	25	E2
Leonard St EC2	32	B2
Leontine Cl SE15	49	E4
Leo St SE15	49	F4
Leroy St SE1	48	C1
Lever St EC1	31	F1
Lewis St NW1	21	F1
Lexham Gdns W8	35	F4
Lexham Gdns Ms W8	35	F4
Lexham Ms W8	43	E1
Lexington St W1	30	A4
Leybourne Rd NW1	21	F2
Liberia Rd N5	23	F1
Library St SE1	39	F3
Liddell Gdns NW10	18	A4
Liddell Rd NW6	19	E1
Lidlington Pl NW1	22	A4
Lilac Pl SE11	47	D1
Lilestone St NW8	28	C2
Lillie Rd SW6	42	C4
Lillie Yd SW6	43	E3
Lily Cl W14	42	C1
Lily Pl EC1	31	E3
Limeburner La EC4	31	F4
Lime Cl E1	41	E2
Lime Gro W12	34	A3
Limerston St SW10	44	A3
Lime St EC3	40	C1
Linacre Ct W6	42	B2
Lincoln's Inn WC2	31	E4
Lincoln's Inn Flds WC2	31	D4
Lincoln St SW3	45	D1
Linden Av NW10	18	B4
Linden Ct W12	34	A2
Linden Gdns W2	35	E1
Lindsay Sq SW1	46	B2
Lindsey Ms N1	24	A2
Lindsey St EC1	31	F3
Linhope St NW1	29	D2
Linsey St SE16	49	E1
Linstead St NW6	19	E2
Linton St N1	24	A3
Lisgar Ter W14	43	D1
Lisle St WC2	38	B1
Lisson Grn Est NW8	28	C2
Lisson Gro NW1	28	C2
Lisson Gro NW8	28	B1
Lisson St NW1	28	C3
Litchfield St WC2	38	B1
Lithos Rd NW3	19	F1
Little Boltons, The SW5	43	F2
Little Boltons, The SW10	43	F2
Little Britain EC1	31	F3
Little Chester St SW1	37	F4
Little Dorrit Ct SE1	40	A3
Little Newport St WC2	38	B1
Little Portland St W1	29	F4
Little Russell St WC1	30	C3
Little St. James's St SW1	38	A2
Livermere Rd E8	25	D3
Liverpool Gro SE17	48	B2
Liverpool Rd N1	23	E4
Liverpool St EC2	32	C3
Lizard St EC1	32	A1
Lloyd Baker St WC1	31	E1
Lloyd's Av EC3	32	C4
Lloyd Sq WC1	31	E1
Lloyd St WC1	31	E1
Lochaline St W6	42	A3
Lockhart Cl N7	23	D1
Lockwood Sq SE16	41	F4
Lodge Rd NW8	28	B1
Loftie St SE16	41	E4
Lofting Rd N1	23	D2
Logan Ms W8	43	E1
Logan Pl W8	43	E1
Lollard St SE11	47	D1
Loman St SE1	39	F3
Lomas Dr E8	25	D2
Lomas St E1	33	E3
Lombard St EC3	32	B4
Lomond Gro SE5	48	B4
Loncroft Rd SE5	48	C3
London Br EC4	40	B2
London Br SE1	40	B2
London Br St SE1	40	B2
London Br Wk SE1	40	B2
London Flds E8	25	F2
London Flds E Side E8	25	F2
London Flds W Side E8	25	E2
London La E8	25	F2
London Rd SE1	39	F4
London Silver Vaults WC2	31	E3
London St W2	28	B4
London Wall EC2	32	A3
Long Acre WC2	38	C1
Longfield Est SE1	49	D1
Longford St NW1	29	F2
Longhope Cl SE15	48	C3
Long La EC1	31	F3
Long La SE1	40	B3
Longley St SE1	49	E1
Longmoore St SW1	46	A1
Longridge Rd SW5	43	E1
Long's Ct WC2	38	B1
Long St E2	33	D1
Long Yd WC1	31	D2
Lonsdale Rd NW6	19	D4
Lonsdale Rd W11	27	D4
Lonsdale Sq N1	23	E2
Lorden Wk E2	33	E1
Lord Hills Rd W2	27	F3
Lord N St SW1	38	C4
Lorenzo St WC1	31	D1
Loris Rd W6	34	A4
Lorne Gdns W11	34	B3
Lorrimore Rd SE17	47	F3
Lorrimore Sq SE17	47	F3
Lothbury EC2	32	B4
Lothrop St W10	26	C1
Lots Rd SW10	44	A4
Loudoun Rd NW8	20	A3
Loughborough St SE11	47	D2
Lough Rd N7	23	D1
Lovegrove St SE1	49	E2
Love La EC2	32	A4
Lovell Ho E8	25	E3
Loveridge Rd NW6	19	D1
Lover's Wk W1	37	E2
Lower Addison Gdns W14	34	C3
Lower Belgrave St SW1	37	F4
Lower Grosvenor Pl SW1	37	F4
Lower Marsh SE1	39	E3
Lower Merton Ri NW3	20	C2
Lower Sloane St SW1	45	E1
Lower Thames St EC3	40	B1
Lowfield Rd NW6	19	E2
Lowndes Cl SW1	37	E4
Lowndes Pl SW1	37	E4
Lowndes Sq SW1	37	D3
Lowndes St SW1	37	D4
Lowther Gdns SW7	36	B3
Lucan Pl SW3	44	C1
Lucey Rd SE16	41	E4
Lucey Way SE16	41	E4
Ludgate Hill EC4	31	F4
Ludgate Sq EC4	31	F4
Luke Ho E1	33	F4
Luke St EC2	32	C2
Lupus St SW1	45	F3
Lurgan Av W6	42	B3
Luscombe Way SW8	46	C4
Luton St NW8	28	B2
Luxborough St W1	29	E2
Luxemburg Gdns W6	42	B1
Lyall Ms SW1	37	E4
Lyall St SW1	37	E4
Lydford Rd NW2	18	B1
Lydford Rd W9	27	D2
Lydney Cl SE15	48	C3
Lyme St NW1	22	A2
Lymington Rd NW6	19	F1
Lympstone Gdns SE15	49	E4
Lynton Rd NW6	19	D3
Lynton Rd SE1	49	D1
Lyons Pl NW8	28	B2
Lyons Wk W14	42	C1
Lysia St SW6	42	B4
Lytham St SE17	48	B2
Lyttelton Cl NW3	20	C2

M

Name	Page	Grid
Mabledon Pl WC1	30	B1
Mablethorpe Rd SW6	42	C4
McAuley Cl SE1	39	E4
Macclesfield Br NW1	20	C4
Macclesfield Rd EC1	32	A1
Macclesfield St W1	38	B1
Macfarlane Rd W12	34	A2
McGregor Rd W11	27	D4
Mackennal St NW8	20	C4
Mackenzie Rd N7	23	D1
Macklin St WC2	30	C4
Macks Rd SE16	49	E1
Mackworth St NW1	30	A1
Macleod St SE17	48	A2
Maclise Rd W14	34	C4
Macroom Rd W9	27	D1
Maddock Way SE17	47	F3
Maddox St W1	37	F1
Madinah Rd E8	25	E1
Madras Pl N7	23	E1
Madrigal La SE5	47	F4
Madron St SE17	48	C2
Magdalen St SE1	40	C2
Magee St SE11	47	E3
Maguire St SE1	41	D3
Maida Av W2	28	A3
Maida Vale W9	19	F4
Maiden La NW1	22	B3
Maiden La WC2	38	C1
Maitland Pk Est NW3	21	D1
Maitland Pk Rd NW3	21	D1
Maitland Pk Vil NW3	21	D1
Makins St SW3	44	C1
Malden Cres NW1	21	E1
Malet Pl WC1	30	B2
Malet St WC1	30	B2

Mal-Mon 65

Name	Page	Grid
Mall, The SW1	38	A3
Mallard Cl NW6	19	E4
Mallord St SW3	44	B3
Malpas Rd E8	25	F1
Maltby St SE1	41	D3
Malt St SE1	49	E3
Malvern Cl W10	27	D3
Malvern Ct SW7	44	B1
Malvern Pl NW6	27	D1
Malvern Rd E8	25	E2
Malvern Rd NW6	27	E1
Malvern Ter N1	23	E3
Manbre Rd W6	42	A3
Manchester Dr W10	26	C2
Manchester Sq W1	29	E4
Manchester St W1	29	E3
Manciple St SE1	40	B4
Mandela St NW1	22	A3
Mandela St SW9	47	E4
Mandela Way SE1	48	C1
Mandeville Pl W1	29	E4
Manette St W1	30	B4
Manger Rd N7	22	C1
Manley St NW1	21	E3
Manor Est SE16	49	D1
Manor Ho Dr NW6	18	B2
Manor Pl SE17	47	F2
Manresa Rd SW3	44	C2
Mansell St E1	33	D4
Mansfield St W1	29	F3
Mansford St E2	25	E4
Mansion Ho EC4	32	B4
Manson Ms SW7	44	A1
Manson Pl SW7	44	B1
Mapesbury Rd NW2	18	C1
Mapeshill Pl NW2	18	A1
Mape St E2	33	F2
Mapledene Rd E8	25	D2
Maple St W1	30	A3
Marban Rd W9	27	D1
Marble Arch W1	37	D1
Marble Quay E1	41	E2
Marchbank Rd W14	43	D3
Marchmont St WC1	30	C2
Marchwood Cl SE5	48	C4
Marcia Rd SE1	48	C1
Marcon Pl E8	25	F1
Marco Rd W6	34	A4
Marden Sq SE16	41	F4
Mare St E8	25	F3
Margaret St W1	29	F4
Margaretta Ter SW3	44	C3
Margery St WC1	31	E1
Margravine Gdns W6	42	B2
Margravine Rd W6	42	B2
Marian Pl E2	25	F4
Marigold St SE16	41	F3
Market Est N7	22	C1
Market Ms W1	37	F2
Market Pl W1	30	A4
Market Rd N7	22	C1
Markham Sq SW3	45	D2
Markham St SW3	44	C2
Markland Ho W10	34	B1
Mark La EC3	40	C1
Marlborough Av E8	25	E3
Marlborough Ct W8	43	E1
Marlborough Gro SE1	49	E2
Marlborough Hill NW8	20	A3
Marlborough Pl NW8	20	A4
Marlborough Rd SW1	38	A2
Marlborough St SW3	44	C1
Marloes Rd W8	35	F4
Marlow Ct NW6	18	B2
Marlowes, The NW8	20	B3
Marne St W10	26	C1
Marquess Rd N1	24	B1
Marquis Rd NW5	21	E1
Marsden St NW5	21	E1
Marshall St W1	30	A4
Marshalsea Rd SE1	40	A3
Marsham St SW1	38	B4
Marsland Cl SE17	47	F2
Marston Cl NW6	20	A2
Martello St E8	25	F2
Martello Ter E8	25	F2
Martha Ct E2	25	F4
Martha St E1	33	F4
Marville Rd SW6	43	D4
Mary Grn NW8	19	F3
Marylands Rd W9	27	E2
Marylebone High St W1	29	E3
Marylebone La W1	29	E4
Marylebone Ms W1	29	F3
Marylebone Rd NW1	28	C3
Marylebone St W1	29	E3
Marylee Way SE11	47	D1
Mary Pl W11	34	C1
Mary St N1	24	A3
Mary Ter NW1	21	F3
Masbro Rd W14	34	B4
Mason's Pl EC1	31	F1
Mason St SE17	48	B1
Masterman Ho SE5	48	B4
Masters Dr SE16	49	F2
Matheson Rd W14	43	D1
Matilda St N1	23	D3
Matthew Cl W10	26	B2
Matthew Parker St SW1	38	B3
Maunsel St SW1	46	B1
Mawbey Est SE1	49	E2
Mawbey Pl SE1	49	D2
Mawbey St SW8	46	C4
Maxwell Rd SW6	43	F4
Mayfair Pl W1	37	F2
Mayfield Rd E8	25	D2
Maygood St N1	23	D4
Maygrove Rd NW6	19	D1
Mazenod Av NW6	19	E2
Meadcroft Rd SE11	47	F3
Meadowbank NW3	21	D2
Meadowbank Cl SW6	42	A4
Meadow Ms SW8	47	D3
Meadow Pl SW8	46	C4
Meadow Rd SW8	47	D3
Meadow Row SE1	40	A4
Meakin Est SE1	40	C4
Meard St W1	30	B4
Mecklenburgh Pl WC1	31	D2
Mecklenburgh Sq WC1	31	D2
Medburn St NW1	22	B4
Medley Rd NW6	19	E1
Medway St SW1	38	B4
Melbourne Pl WC2	39	D1
Melbury Ct W8	35	D4
Melbury Rd W14	35	D4
Melcombe Pl NW1	29	D3
Melcombe St NW1	29	D2
Melina Pl NW8	28	B1
Melior St SE1	40	B3
Melrose Gdns W6	34	A4
Melrose Ter W6	34	A3
Melton Ct SW7	44	B1
Melton St NW1	30	B1
Mendora Rd SW6	42	C4
Mentmore Ter E8	25	F2
Mepham St SE1	39	D2
Merceron St E1	33	F2
Mercers Pl W6	42	A1
Mercer St WC2	30	C4
Mermaid Ct SE1	40	B3
Merrick Sq SE1	40	A4
Merrington Rd SW6	43	E3
Merrow St SE17	48	A3
Merton Ri NW3	20	C2
Messina Av NW6	19	E2
Methley St SE11	47	E2
Methwold Rd W10	26	B3
Mews Deck E1	41	F1
Mews St E1	41	E2
Meymott St SE1	39	F2
Micawber St N1	32	A1
Micklethwaite Rd SW6	43	E3
Middle Row W10	26	C2
Middlesex St E1	32	C3
Middle Temple La EC4	31	E4
Middleton Rd E8	25	D2
Middleton St E2	33	F1
Midland Rd NW1	22	B4
Milborne Gro SW10	44	A2
Milcote St SE1	39	F3
Mildmay Av N1	24	B1
Mildmay St N1	24	B1
Miles St SW8	46	C3
Milford La WC2	39	D1
Millbank SW1	38	C4
Millbank Twr SW1	46	C1
Millennium Br EC4	40	A1
Millennium Br SE1	40	A1
Millennium Pl E2	25	F4
Miller St NW1	22	A4
Millers Way W6	34	A3
Miller Wk SE1	39	E2
Millman Ms WC1	31	D2
Millman St WC1	31	D2
Mill Row N1	24	C3
Mill Shot Cl SW6	42	A4
Millstream Rd SE1	41	D3
Mill St SE1	41	D3
Mill St W1	38	A1
Milman Rd NW6	18	C4
Milman's St SW10	44	B3
Milner Pl N1	23	E3
Milner Sq N1	23	F2
Milner St SW3	45	D1
Milson Rd W14	34	C4
Milton Cl SE1	49	D1
Milton St EC2	32	B3
Milverton Rd NW6	18	A2
Milverton St SE11	47	E2
Mina Rd SE17	48	C2
Mincing La EC3	40	C1
Minera Ms SW1	45	E1
Minerva Cl SW9	47	E4
Minerva St E2	25	F4
Minford Gdns W14	34	B3
Minories EC3	33	D4
Mintern St N1	24	B4
Mirabel Rd SW6	43	D4
Mitchell St EC1	32	A2
Mitchison Rd N1	24	B1
Mitre Rd SE1	39	E3
Mitre St EC3	32	C4
Molyneux St W1	28	C3
Monck St SW1	38	B4
Monkton St SE11	47	E1
Monmouth Rd W2	27	F4
Monmouth St WC2	38	C1
Monnow Rd SE1	49	D2
Montague Cl SE1	40	B2

Name	Page	Grid
Montague Pl WC1	30	B3
Montague St EC1	32	A4
Montague St WC1	30	C3
Montagu Ms N W1	29	D3
Montagu Pl W1	29	D3
Montagu Sq W1	29	D3
Montagu St W1	29	D4
Montford Pl SE11	47	E2
Montpelier Pl SW7	36	C4
Montpelier Sq SW7	36	C3
Montpelier St SW7	36	C3
Montpelier Wk SW7	36	C4
Montrose Av NW6	18	C4
Montrose Ct SW7	36	B3
Montrose Pl SW1	37	E3
Monument St EC3	40	B1
Moody Rd SE15	49	D4
Moon St N1	23	F3
Moore Pk Rd SW6	43	F4
Moore St SW3	45	D1
Moorfields EC2	32	B3
Moorgate EC2	32	B4
Moorhouse Rd W2	27	E4
Moor La EC2	32	B3
Mora St EC1	32	A1
Morecambe St SE17	48	A1
More Cl W14	42	C1
Moreland St EC1	31	F1
Moreton Pl SW1	46	A2
Moreton St SW1	46	B2
Moreton Ter SW1	46	A2
Morgan Rd W10	27	D3
Morgans La SE1	40	C2
Morley St SE1	39	E3
Mornington Av W14	43	D1
Mornington Cres NW1	22	A4
Mornington St NW1	21	F4
Mornington Ter NW1	21	F3
Morocco St SE1	40	C3
Morpeth Ter SW1	38	A4
Morris St E1	33	F4
Morshead Rd W9	27	E1
Mortimer Cres NW6	19	F3
Mortimer Est NW6	19	F3
Mortimer Pl NW6	19	F3
Mortimer Rd N1	24	C2
Mortimer Rd NW10	26	A1
Mortimer St W1	29	F4
Morton Rd N1	24	A2
Moscow Rd W2	35	E1
Mossop St SW3	44	C1
Mostyn Gdns NW10	18	B4
Motcomb St SW1	37	E4
Mount Pleasant WC1	31	E2
Mount Pleasant Rd NW10	18	A2
Mount Row W1	37	F1
Mount St W1	37	E1
Mowbray Rd NW6	18	C2
Mowlem St E2	25	F4
Mowll St SW9	47	E4
Moxon St W1	29	E3
Moylan Rd W6	42	C3
Mozart St W10	27	D1
Mozart Ter SW1	45	E1
Mulberry Rd E8	25	D2
Mulberry Wk SW3	44	B3
Mulgrave Rd SW6	43	D3
Mulvaney Way SE1	40	B3
Munden St W14	42	C1
Mund St W14	43	D2
Mundy St N1	32	C1
Munro Ms W10	26	C3
Munro Ter SW10	44	B4
Munster Sq NW1	29	F1
Munton Rd SE17	48	A1
Murdock St SE15	49	F3
Muriel St N1	23	D4
Murphy St SE1	39	E3
Murray Gro N1	24	A4
Murray Ms NW1	22	B2
Murray St NW1	22	B2
Musard Rd W6	42	C3
Musard Rd W14	42	C3
Muscal W6	42	C3
Museum St WC1	30	C4
Mutrix Rd NW6	19	E3
Myddelton Sq EC1	31	E1
Myddelton St EC1	31	E1
Mylne St EC1	31	E1
Myrdle St E1	33	E3
Myrtle Wk N1	24	C4

N

Name	Page	Grid
N1 Shop Cen N1	23	E4
Napier Gro N1	24	A4
Napier Pl W14	35	D4
Napier Rd W14	35	D4
Napier Ter N1	23	F2
Nascot St W12	26	A4
Naseby Cl NW6	20	A2
Nassau St W1	30	A3
Navarino Gro E8	25	E1
Navarino Rd E8	25	E1
Navarre St E2	33	D2
Naylor Rd SE15	49	F4
Nazrul St E2	33	D1
Neal St WC2	30	C4
Neate St SE5	49	D3
Nebraska St SE1	40	A3
Neckinger SE16	41	D4
Neckinger Est SE16	41	D3
Neckinger St SE1	41	D3
Nella Rd W6	42	B3
Nelson Cl NW6	19	E4
Nelson Gdns E2	33	E1
Nelson Pl N1	23	F4
Nelson Sq SE1	39	F3
Nelson St E1	33	F4
Nelson Ter N1	23	F4
Nesham St E1	41	E2
Netherhall Gdns NW3	20	A1
Netherton Gro SW10	44	A3
Netherwood Rd W14	34	B4
Netherwood St NW6	19	D2
Nevern Pl SW5	43	E1
Nevern Rd SW5	43	E1
Nevern Sq SW5	43	E1
Neville Cl NW6	19	D4
Neville Cl SE15	49	E4
Neville Rd NW6	19	D4
Neville St SW7	44	B2
Neville Ter SW7	44	B2
Newark St E1	33	F3
New Bond St W1	37	F1
New Br St EC4	31	F4
New Broad St EC2	32	C3
Newburgh St W1	30	A4
New Burlington St W1	38	A1
Newburn St SE11	47	D2
Newcastle Pl W2	28	B3
New Cavendish St W1	29	E3
New Change EC4	32	A4
New Ch Rd SE5	48	A4
Newcomen St SE1	40	B3
New Compton St WC2	30	B4
Newcourt St NW8	20	C4
New Covent Gdn Mkt SW8	46	B4
Newent Cl SE15	48	C4
New Fetter La EC4	31	E4
Newgate St EC1	31	F4
New Globe Wk SE1	40	A2
Newington Butts SE1	47	F1
Newington Butts SE11	47	F1
Newington Causeway SE1	39	F4
Newington Grn Rd N1	24	B1
New Inn Yd EC2	32	C2
New Kent Rd SE1	40	A4
Newman St W1	30	A3
New N Rd N1	24	B4
New N St WC1	31	D3
New Oxford St WC1	30	B4
New Pl Sq SE16	41	F4
Newport Pl WC2	38	B1
Newport St SE11	47	D1
New Quebec St W1	29	D4
New Ride SW7	36	C3
New River Wk N1	24	A1
New Rd E1	33	F3
New Row WC2	38	C1
New Sq WC2	31	D4
New St EC2	32	C3
Newton Rd W2	27	E4
Newton St WC2	30	C4
New Union St EC2	32	B3
New Wf Rd N1	22	C4
Nicholl St E2	25	E3
Nicholson St SE1	39	F2
Nightingale Rd N1	24	A1
Nile St N1	32	B1
Nile Ter SE15	49	D2
Nine Elms La SW8	46	A4
Niton St SW6	42	B4
Noble St EC2	32	A4
Noel Rd N1	23	F4
Noel St W1	30	A4
Norfolk Cres W2	28	C4
Norfolk Pl W2	28	B4
Norfolk Rd NW8	20	B3
Norfolk Sq W2	28	B4
Norland Ho W11	34	B2
Norland Pl W11	34	C2
Norland Rd W11	34	B2
Norland Sq W11	34	C2
Normand Rd W14	43	D3
Northampton Pk N1	24	A1
Northampton Rd EC1	31	E2
Northampton Sq EC1	31	F1
Northampton St N1	24	A2
North Audley St W1	29	E4
North Bk NW8	28	C1
Northburgh St EC1	31	F2
North Carriage Dr W2	36	C1
Northchurch Rd N1	24	B2
Northchurch Ter N1	24	C2
North Cres WC1	30	B3
Northdown St N1	23	D4
North End Cres W14	43	D1
North End Ho W14	42	C1
North End Rd SW6	43	D3
North End Rd W14	42	C1
North Gower St NW1	30	A1
Northiam St E9	25	F3
Northington St WC1	31	D2
North Ms WC1	31	D2
North Peckham Est SE15	49	D4
North Pole Rd W10	26	A3
Northport St N1	24	B3
North Ride W2	36	C1
North Rd N7	22	C1

Nor-Pas 67

Name	Page	Grid
North Row W1	37	D1
North Tenter St E1	33	D4
North Ter SW3	36	C4
Northumberland All EC3	32	C4
Northumberland Av WC2	38	C2
Northumberland Pl W2	27	E4
Northumberland St WC2	38	C2
North Vil NW1	22	B1
North Wf Rd W2	28	B3
Northwick Ter NW8	28	B2
Norton Folgate E1	32	C3
Norwich St EC4	31	E4
Notley St SE5	48	B4
Notting Barn Rd W10	26	B2
Nottingham Pl W1	29	E2
Nottingham St W1	29	E3
Notting Hill Gate W11	35	E2
Nugent Ter NW8	20	A4
Nursery La E2	25	D3
Nursery La W10	26	A3
Nutbourne St W10	26	C1
Nutcroft Rd SE15	49	F4
Nutford Pl W1	29	D4
Nutley Ter NW3	20	A1
Nuttall St N1	24	C4
Nutt St SE15	49	D4

O

Name	Page	Grid
Oakden St SE11	47	E1
Oakey La SE1	39	E4
Oakfield St SW10	44	A3
Oakington Rd W9	27	E2
Oakley Gdns SW3	44	C3
Oakley Pl SE1	49	D2
Oakley Rd N1	24	B2
Oakley Sq NW1	22	A4
Oakley St SW3	44	C3
Oakley Wk W6	42	B3
Oak Tree Rd NW8	28	C1
Oakwood Ct W14	35	D4
Oakwood La W14	35	D4
Oakworth Rd W10	26	A3
Oat La EC2	32	A4
Observatory Gdns W8	35	E3
Occupation Rd SE17	48	A2
Ockendon Rd N1	24	B1
Offley Rd SW9	47	E4
Offord Rd N1	23	D2
Offord St N1	23	D2
Ogle St W1	30	A3
Okehampton Rd NW10	18	A3
Olaf St W11	34	B1
Old Bailey EC4	31	F4
Old Bethnal Grn Rd E2	33	E1
Old Bond St W1	38	A1
Old Broad St EC2	32	B4
Old Brompton Rd SW5	43	E2
Old Brompton Rd SW7	43	E2
Old Burlington St W1	38	A1
Oldbury Pl W1	29	E2
Old Castle St E1	33	D3
Old Cavendish St W1	29	F4
Old Ch St SW3	44	B2
Old Compton St W1	38	B1
Old Ct Pl W8	35	F3
Old Gloucester St WC1	30	C3
Old Jamaica Rd SE16	41	E4
Old Jewry EC2	32	B4
Old Kent Rd SE1	48	C1
Old Kent Rd SE15	48	C1
Old Marylebone Rd NW1	28	C3
Old Montague St E1	33	E3
Old Nichol St E2	33	D2
Old Palace Yd SW1	38	C4
Old Paradise St SE11	47	D1
Old Pk La W1	37	E2
Old Pye St SW1	38	B4
Old Quebec St W1	29	D4
Old Queen St SW1	38	B3
Old Royal Free Sq N1	23	E3
Old S Lambeth Rd SW8	46	C4
Old Spitalfields Mkt E1	33	D3
Old Sq WC2	31	E4
Old St EC1	32	A2
Oliphant St W10	26	B1
Olmar St SE1	49	E3
Olney Rd SE17	47	F3
Olympia Way W14	34	C4
O'Meara St SE1	40	A2
Ongar Rd SW6	43	E3
Onslow Gdns SW7	44	B2
Onslow Sq SW7	44	B1
Ontario St SE1	39	F4
Opal St SE11	47	F1
Oppidans Rd NW3	21	D2
Orange St WC2	38	B1
Oransay Rd N1	24	A1
Orbain Rd SW6	42	C4
Orb St SE17	48	B1
Orchard Cl W10	26	C3
Orchardson St NW8	28	B2
Orchard St W1	29	E4
Orde Hall St WC1	31	D2
Ordnance Hill NW8	20	B3
Orleston Ms N7	23	E1
Orleston Rd N7	23	E1
Orme Ct W2	35	F1
Orme La W2	35	F1
Ormonde Gate SW3	45	D2
Ormonde Ter NW8	21	D3
Ormsby St E2	25	D4
Orsett St SE11	47	D2
Orsett Ter W2	28	A4
Orsman Rd N1	24	C3
Osborn Cl E8	25	E3
Osborn St E1	33	D3
Oseney Cres NW5	22	A1
Osnaburgh St NW1	29	F2
Osnaburgh St (north section) NW1	29	F1
Osric Path N1	24	C4
Ossington St W2	35	E1
Ossory Rd SE1	49	E2
Ossulston St NW1	30	B1
Oswell Ho E1	41	F2
Oswin St SE11	47	F1
Otterburn Ho SE5	48	A4
Otto St SE17	47	F3
Outer Circle NW1	21	F4
Outram Pl N1	22	C3
Oval, The E2	25	F4
Oval Pl SW8	47	D4
Oval Rd NW1	21	F3
Oval Way SE11	47	D2
Oversley Ho W2	27	E3
Overstone Rd W6	34	A4
Ovington Gdns SW3	36	C4
Ovington Ms SW3	36	C4
Ovington Sq SW3	36	C4
Ovington St SW3	36	C4
Oxendon St SW1	38	B1
Oxenholme NW1	22	A4
Oxford Gdns W10	26	C4
Oxford Gate W6	42	B1
Oxford Rd NW6	19	E4
Oxford Sq W2	28	C4
Oxford St W1	29	F4
Oxley Cl SE1	49	D2
Oxo Twr Wf SE1	39	E1

P

Name	Page	Grid
Packington Sq N1	24	A3
Packington St N1	23	F3
Padbury SE17	48	C2
Padbury Ct E2	33	D1
Paddington Grn W2	28	B3
Paddington St W1	29	E3
Page St SW1	46	B1
Pages Wk SE1	48	C1
Pakenham St WC1	31	D1
Palace Av W8	35	F2
Palace Ct W2	35	F1
Palace Gdns Ms W8	35	E2
Palace Gdns Ter W8	35	E2
Palace Gate W8	36	A3
Palace Grn W8	35	F3
Palace St SW1	38	A4
Palfrey Pl SW8	47	D4
Palgrave Gdns NW1	28	C2
Palliser Rd W14	42	C2
Pall Mall SW1	38	A2
Pall Mall E SW1	38	B2
Palmerston Rd NW6	19	E2
Palmer St SW1	38	B4
Pancras Rd NW1	22	B4
Pandora Rd NW6	19	E1
Pangbourne Av W10	26	A3
Parade, The SW11	45	D4
Paradise St SE16	41	F3
Paradise Wk SW3	45	D3
Pardoner St SE1	40	B4
Parfett St E1	33	E3
Parfrey St W6	42	A3
Paris Gdn SE1	39	F2
Park Cl SW1	37	D3
Park Cl W14	35	D4
Park Cres W1	29	F2
Parker St WC2	30	C4
Parkgate Rd SW11	44	C4
Parkholme Rd E8	25	D1
Parkhouse St SE5	48	B4
Park La W1	37	E1
Park Pl SW1	38	A2
Park Pl Vil W2	28	A3
Park Rd NW1	28	C1
Park Rd NW8	28	C1
Park Sq E NW1	29	F2
Park Sq Ms NW1	29	F2
Park Sq W NW1	29	F2
Park St SE1	40	A2
Park St W1	37	E1
Park Village E NW1	21	F4
Park Village W NW1	21	F4
Parkville Rd SW6	43	D4
Park Wk SW10	44	A3
Parkway NW1	21	F3
Parliament Sq SW1	38	C3
Parliament St SW1	38	C3
Parliament Vw Apartments SE1	47	D1
Parmiter St E2	25	F4
Parr St N1	24	B4
Parry Rd W10	26	C1
Parry St SW8	46	C3
Parson's Ho W2	28	B2
Pascal St SW8	46	B4
Passmore St SW1	45	E1
Pastor St SE11	47	F1

Street	Page	Grid
Pater St W8	35	E4
Patmos Rd SW9	47	F4
Patriot Sq E2	25	F4
Patshull Rd NW5	22	A1
Paul St EC2	32	B2
Paul's Wk EC4	40	A1
Paultons Sq SW3	44	B3
Paultons St SW3	44	B3
Paveley Dr SW11	44	C4
Paveley St NW8	28	C2
Pavilion Rd SW1	37	D3
Paxton Ter SW1	45	F3
Paynes Wk W6	42	C3
Peabody Est W10	26	A3
Peabody Sq SE1	39	F3
Peabody Trust SE1	40	A2
Peach Rd W10	26	B1
Pearman St SE1	39	E3
Pearson St E2	24	C4
Pear Tree Cl E2	25	D3
Pear Tree Ct EC1	31	E2
Pear Tree St EC1	31	F2
Peckham Gro SE15	48	C4
Peckham Hill St SE15	49	E4
Peckham Pk Rd SE15	49	E4
Pedlars Wk N7	22	C1
Pedley St E1	33	D2
Peel Prec NW6	19	E4
Peel Rd NW6	27	D1
Peel St W8	35	E2
Peerless St EC1	32	B1
Pelham Cres SW7	44	C1
Pelham Pl SW7	44	C1
Pelham St SW7	44	C1
Pellant Rd SW6	42	C4
Pelter St E2	33	D1
Pember Rd NW10	26	B1
Pembridge Cres W11	35	E1
Pembridge Gdns W2	35	E1
Pembridge Ms W11	35	E1
Pembridge Pl W2	35	E1
Pembridge Rd W11	35	E1
Pembridge Sq W2	35	E1
Pembridge Vil W2	35	E1
Pembridge Vil W11	35	E1
Pembroke Av N1	22	C2
Pembroke Cl SW1	37	E3
Pembroke Gdns W8	43	D1
Pembroke Gdns Cl W8	35	E4
Pembroke Pl W8	35	E4
Pembroke Rd W8	43	E1
Pembroke Sq W8	35	E4
Pembroke St N1	22	C2
Pembroke Studios W8	35	D4
Pembroke Vil W8	43	E1
Pembroke Wk W8	43	E1
Penang St E1	41	F2
Pencraig Way SE15	49	F3
Penfold Pl NW1	28	C3
Penfold St NW1	28	B2
Penfold St NW8	28	B2
Pennack Rd SE15	49	D3
Pennant Ms W8	43	F1
Pennard Rd W12	34	A3
Pennethorne Rd SE15	49	F4
Pennington St E1	41	E1
Penn St N1	24	B3
Penpoll Rd E8	25	F1
Penrose Gro SE17	48	A2
Penrose Ho SE17	48	A2
Penrose St SE17	48	A2
Penryn St NW1	22	B4
Penton Pl SE17	47	F2
Penton Ri WC1	31	D1
Penton St N1	23	E4
Pentonville Rd N1	23	D4
Pentridge St SE15	49	D4
Penywern Rd SW5	43	E2
Penzance Pl W11	34	C2
Penzance St W11	34	C2
Peploe Rd NW6	18	B4
Pepys St EC3	40	C1
Percival St EC1	31	F2
Percy Circ WC1	31	D1
Percy St W1	30	B3
Peregrine Ho EC1	31	F1
Perham Rd W14	42	C2
Perkin's Rents SW1	38	B4
Perseverance Pl SW9	47	E4
Petersham La SW7	36	A4
Petersham Ms SW7	36	A4
Petersham Pl SW7	36	A4
Peter St W1	38	B1
Petley Rd W6	42	A3
Peto Pl NW1	29	F2
Petrie Ms NW2	18	C1
Petticoat La E1	32	C3
Petticoat Sq E1	33	D4
Petty France SW1	38	A4
Petyward SW3	44	C1
Phelp St SE17	48	B3
Phene St SW3	44	C3
Philbeach Gdns SW5	43	E2
Phillimore Gdns NW10	18	A3
Phillimore Gdns W8	35	E3
Phillimore Pl W8	35	E3
Phillimore Wk W8	35	E4
Phillipp St N1	24	C3
Philpot St E1	33	F4
Phipp St EC2	32	C2
Phoenix Pl WC1	31	D2
Phoenix Rd NW1	30	B1
Piccadilly W1	37	F2
Piccadilly Circ W1	38	B1
Pickfords Wf N1	24	A4
Picton St SE5	48	B4
Pilgrimage St SE1	40	B3
Pilton Pl SE17	48	A2
Pimlico Rd SW1	45	E2
Pinchin St E1	41	E1
Pindar St EC2	32	C3
Pine St EC1	31	E2
Piper Cl N7	23	D1
Pitfield Est N1	32	B1
Pitfield St N1	32	C1
Pitman St SE5	48	A4
Pitt's Head Ms W1	37	E2
Pitt St W8	35	E3
Platt St NW1	22	B4
Plaza Shop Cen, The W1	30	A4
Pleasant Pl N1	23	F2
Pleasant Row NW1	21	F3
Plender St NW1	22	A3
Plough Yd EC2	32	C2
Plumbers Row E1	33	E3
Plympton Av NW6	19	D2
Plympton Rd NW6	19	D2
Plympton St NW8	28	C2
Pocock St SE1	39	F3
Poland St W1	30	A4
Polesworth Ho W2	27	E3
Pollard Row E2	33	E1
Pollard St E2	33	E1
Polygon Rd NW1	22	B4
Pond Pl SW3	44	C1
Ponler St E1	33	F4
Ponsonby Pl SW1	46	B2
Ponsonby Ter SW1	46	B2
Ponton Rd SW8	46	B3
Pont St SW1	37	D4
Pont St Ms SW1	37	D4
Poole St N1	24	B3
Pope St SE1	40	C3
Popham Rd N1	24	A3
Popham St N1	23	F3
Poplar Gro W6	34	A4
Poplar Pl W2	35	F1
Porchester Gdns W2	35	F1
Porchester Ms W2	27	F4
Porchester Pl W2	28	C4
Porchester Rd W2	27	F3
Porchester Sq W2	27	F4
Porchester Ter W2	36	A1
Porchester Ter N W2	27	F4
Porlock St SE1	40	B3
Porten Rd W14	34	C4
Porteus Rd W2	28	A3
Portgate Cl W9	27	D2
Portland Pl W1	29	F3
Portland Rd W11	34	C1
Portland St SE17	48	B2
Portman Cl W1	29	D4
Portman Ms S W1	29	E4
Portman Sq W1	29	D4
Portman St W1	29	E4
Portnall Rd W9	19	D4
Portobello Rd W10	27	D4
Portobello Rd W11	27	D4
Portpool La EC1	31	E3
Portsoken St E1	41	D1
Portugal St WC2	31	D4
Post Office Way SW8	46	B4
Potier St SE1	40	B4
Pottery St SE16	41	F3
Pott St E2	33	F1
Poultry EC2	32	B4
Powis Gdns W11	27	D4
Powis Pl WC1	30	C2
Powis Sq W11	27	D4
Powis Ter W11	27	D4
Pownall Rd E8	25	D3
Poynter Ho W11	34	B2
Poyser St E2	25	F4
Praed St W2	28	B4
Pratt St NW1	22	A3
Pratt Wk SE11	47	D1
Prebend St N1	24	A3
Prescot St E1	41	D1
Price's St SE1	39	F2
Price's Yd N1	23	D3
Prideaux Pl WC1	31	D1
Prima Rd SW9	47	E4
Primrose Gdns NW3	20	C1
Primrose Hill Ct NW3	21	D2
Primrose Hill Rd NW3	20	C2
Primrose St EC2	32	C3
Prince Albert Rd NW1	20	C4
Prince Albert Rd NW8	20	C4
Prince Consort Rd SW7	36	A4
Princedale Rd W11	34	C2
Princelet St E1	33	D3
Prince of Wales Dr SW8	45	F4
Prince of Wales Gate SW7	36	C3
Prince of Wales Rd NW5	21	E1
Princes Ct E1	41	E1
Princes Gdns SW7	36	B4
Princes Gate SW7	36	C3
Princes Gate Ms SW7	36	B4
Princes Pl W11	34	C2
Princes Sq W2	35	F1

Pri-Rod 69

Name	Page	Grid
Princess Rd NW1	21	E3
Princess Rd NW6	19	E4
Princess St SE1	39	F4
Princes St EC2	32	B4
Princes St W1	29	F4
Princethorpe Ho W2	27	F3
Princeton St WC1	31	D3
Prior Bolton St N1	23	F1
Prioress St SE1	40	B4
Priory Grn Est N1	23	D4
Priory Pk Rd NW6	19	D3
Priory Rd NW6	19	F3
Priory Ter NW6	19	F3
Priory Wk SW10	44	A2
Pritchard's Rd E2	25	E3
Priter Rd SE16	41	E4
Procter St WC1	31	D3
Prothero Rd SW6	42	C4
Providence Ct W1	37	E1
Provost Est N1	24	B4
Provost Rd NW3	21	D2
Provost St N1	32	B1
Prusom St E1	41	F2
Pudding La EC3	40	B1
Pulteney Ter N1	23	D3
Pulton Pl SW6	43	E4
Pundersons Gdns E2	33	F1
Purbrook St SE1	40	C4
Purcell Cres SW6	42	C4
Purcell St N1	24	C4
Purchese St NW1	22	B4
Purves Rd NW10	18	A4

Q

Name	Page	Grid
Quaker St E1	33	D2
Quality Ct WC2	31	E4
Queen Anne's Gate SW1	38	B3
Queen Anne St W1	29	F4
Queen Caroline Est W6	42	A2
Queen Caroline St W6	42	A1
Queen Elizabeth St SE1	41	D3
Queenhithe EC4	40	A1
Queensberry Pl SW7	44	B1
Queensborough Ter W2	35	F1
Queensbridge Rd E2	25	D3
Queensbridge Rd E8	25	D2
Queensbury St N1	24	A2
Queens Club Gdns W14	42	C3
Queen's Cres NW5	21	E1
Queensdale Cres W11	34	B2
Queensdale Pl W11	34	C2
Queensdale Rd W11	34	B2
Queensdale Wk W11	34	C2
Queens Gdns W2	36	A1
Queen's Gate SW7	44	B1
Queen's Gate Gdns SW7	36	A4
Queen's Gate Ms SW7	36	A3
Queensgate Pl NW6	19	E2
Queen's Gate Pl SW7	36	A4
Queen's Gate Pl Ms SW7	36	A4
Queen's Gate Ter SW7	36	A4
Queen's Gro NW8	20	B3
Queen's Gro Ms NW8	20	B3
Queen's Head St N1	23	F3
Queensmead NW8	20	B3
Queens Ms W2	35	F1
Queensmill Rd SW6	42	B4
Queens Pk Ct W10	26	B1
Queen Sq WC1	30	C2
Queen's Row SE17	48	B3
Queen's Ter NW8	20	B4
Queenstown Rd SW8	45	E4
Queen St EC4	40	A1
Queen St W1	37	F2
Queen's Wk SE1	40	C2
Queen's Wk SW1	38	A2
Queensway W2	27	F4
Queen Victoria St EC4	39	F1
Quex Rd NW6	19	E3
Quick St N1	23	F4
Quilter St E2	33	E1

R

Name	Page	Grid
Racton Rd SW6	43	E3
Radcot St SE11	47	E2
Raddington Rd W10	26	C3
Radlett Pl NW8	20	C3
Radley Ms W8	35	E4
Radnor Pl W2	28	C4
Radnor Rd NW6	18	C3
Radnor Rd SE15	49	E4
Radnor St EC1	32	A1
Radnor Ter W14	43	D1
Radnor Wk SW3	44	C2
Radstock St SW11	44	C4
Raglan St NW5	21	F1
Railway App SE1	40	B2
Railway St N1	22	C4
Rainbow St SE5	48	C4
Raine St E1	41	F2
Rainham Rd NW10	26	A1
Rainville Rd W6	42	A3
Raleigh St N1	23	F3
Ramillies Pl W1	30	A4
Rampayne St SW1	46	B2
Ramsey St E2	33	E2
Ramsey Wk N1	24	B1
Randall Rd SE11	47	D1
Randell's Rd N1	22	C3
Randolph Av W9	28	A2
Randolph Cres W9	28	A2
Randolph Gdns NW6	19	F4
Randolph Ms W9	28	A2
Randolph Rd W9	28	A2
Randolph St NW1	22	A2
Ranelagh Gro SW1	45	E2
Rannoch Rd W6	42	A3
Raphael St SW7	37	D3
Rathbone Pl W1	30	B4
Rathbone St W1	30	A3
Raven Row E1	33	F3
Ravenscroft St E2	25	D4
Ravensdon St SE11	47	E2
Ravenstone SE17	48	C2
Rawlings St SW3	45	D1
Rawstorne St EC1	31	F1
Raymouth Rd SE16	49	F1
Ray St EC1	31	E2
Reading La E8	25	F1
Reardon Path E1	41	F2
Reardon St E1	41	F2
Rector St N1	24	A3
Redan Pl W2	27	F4
Redan St W14	34	B4
Redbridge Gdns SE5	48	C4
Redburn St SW3	45	D3
Redcar St SE5	48	A4
Redchurch St E2	33	D2
Redcliffe Gdns SW5	43	F2
Redcliffe Gdns SW10	43	F2
Redcliffe Ms SW10	43	F2
Redcliffe Pl SW10	44	A3
Redcliffe Rd SW10	44	A2
Redcliffe Sq SW10	43	F2
Redcliffe St SW10	43	F3
Redcross Way SE1	40	A3
Reddins Rd SE15	49	E3
Redesdale St SW3	45	D3
Redfield La SW5	43	E1
Redhill St NW1	21	F4
Red Lion Row SE17	48	A3
Red Lion Sq WC1	31	D3
Red Lion St WC1	31	D3
Reece Ms SW7	44	B1
Reedworth St SE11	47	E1
Rees St N1	24	A3
Reeves Ms W1	37	E1
Regan Way N1	24	C4
Regency St SW1	46	B1
Regents Br Gdns SW8	46	C4
Regent's Pk NW1	21	E4
Regents Pk Rd NW1	21	D3
Regent Sq WC1	30	C1
Regents Row E8	25	E3
Regent St SW1	38	B1
Regent St W1	29	F4
Relay Rd W12	34	A1
Remington St N1	23	F4
Renfrew Rd SE11	47	F1
Rennie Est SE16	49	F1
Rennie St SE1	39	F2
Reverdy Rd SE1	49	E1
Rewell St SW6	44	A4
Rheidol Ter N1	23	F4
Rhyl St NW5	21	E1
Richborne Ter SW8	47	D4
Richford St W6	34	A3
Richmond Av N1	23	D3
Richmond Av NW10	18	A1
Richmond Cres N1	23	D3
Richmond Gro N1	23	F2
Richmond Rd E8	25	D2
Richmond Ter SW1	38	C3
Richmond Way W12	34	A3
Richmond Way W14	34	B4
Rickett St SW6	43	E3
Riding Ho St W1	29	F3
Rifle Pl SE11	47	E3
Riley Rd SE1	41	D4
Riley St SW10	44	B3
Ring, The W2	36	B1
Ring Rd W12	34	A1
Ripplevale Gro N1	23	D2
Risinghill St N1	23	D4
Rita Rd SW8	47	D4
Ritchie St N1	23	E4
Ritson Rd E8	25	E1
River Pl N1	24	A2
Riverside Ct SW8	46	B3
River St EC1	31	E1
Riverton Cl W9	27	D2
Rivington St EC2	32	C1
Robert Adam St W1	29	E4
Roberta St E2	33	E1
Robert Dashwood Way SE17	48	A2
Robert St NW1	29	F1
Robin Ct SE16	49	E1
Rochester Ms NW1	22	A1
Rochester Pl NW1	22	A1
Rochester Rd NW1	22	A1
Rochester Row SW1	46	A1
Rochester Sq NW1	22	A2
Rochester St SW1	38	B4
Rochester Ter NW1	22	A1
Rockingham Est SE1	40	A4
Rockingham St SE1	40	A4
Rockley Rd W14	34	B3
Rockwood Pl W12	34	A3
Rodmarton St W1	29	D3

70 Rod-St. Q

Name	Page	Grid
Rodney Pl SE17	48	A1
Rodney Rd SE17	48	A1
Rodney St N1	23	D4
Roger St WC1	31	D2
Roland Gdns SW7	44	A2
Roland Way SE17	48	B2
Rolls Rd SE1	49	D2
Roman Way N7	23	D1
Romford St E1	33	E3
Romilly St W1	38	B1
Romney St SW1	38	B4
Rood La EC3	40	C1
Rootes Dr W10	26	B2
Ropemaker St EC2	32	B3
Ropley St E2	25	E4
Rosaline Rd SW6	42	C4
Rosary Gdns SW7	44	A1
Rosaville Rd SW6	43	D4
Rose All SE1	40	A2
Roseberry Pl E8	25	D1
Roseberry St SE16	49	F1
Rosebery Av EC1	31	E2
Rosedene NW6	18	B3
Rosedew Rd W6	42	B3
Roseford St W12	34	B3
Rosemary Rd SE15	49	D4
Rosemont Rd NW3	20	A1
Rosemoor St SW3	45	D1
Rose Sq SW3	44	B2
Rosetta Cl SW8	46	C4
Rosmead Rd W11	34	C1
Rosoman St EC1	31	E1
Rossendale Way NW1	22	A2
Rossetti Rd SE16	49	F2
Rossmore Rd NW1	28	C2
Rotherfield St N1	24	A2
Rotherhithe New Rd SE16	49	E2
Rothery Ter SW9	47	F4
Rothsay St SE1	40	C4
Rothwell St NW1	21	D3
Rotten Row SW1	37	D3
Rotten Row SW7	36	C3
Rouel Rd SE16	41	E4
Roupell St SE1	39	E2
Rousden St NW1	22	A2
Rowallan Rd SW6	42	C4
Rowan Rd W6	42	B1
Rowberry Cl SW6	42	A4
Rowcross St SE1	49	D2
Rowington Cl W2	27	F3
Rowley Way NW8	19	F3
Roxby Pl SW6	43	E3
Royal Av SW3	45	D2
Royal Coll St NW1	22	A2
Royal Cres W11	34	B2
Royal Ex EC3	32	B4
Royal Hosp Rd SW3	45	D3
Royal Ms, The SW1	37	F4
Royal Mint Ct EC3	41	D1
Royal Mint St E1	41	D1
Royal Oak Rd E8	25	F1
Royal Opera Arc SW1	38	B2
Royal Rd SE17	47	F3
Royal St SE1	39	D4
Rozel Ct N1	24	C3
Ruby St SE15	49	F3
Rudolph Rd NW6	19	E4
Rufford St N1	22	C3
Rugby St WC1	31	D2
Rumbold Rd SW6	43	F4
Runcorn Pl W11	34	C1
Rupert Rd NW6	19	D4
Rupert St W1	38	B1
Rushton St N1	24	B4
Rushworth St SE1	39	F3
Russell Gdns W14	34	C4
Russell Gdns Ms W14	34	C4
Russell Gro SW9	47	E4
Russell Rd W14	34	C4
Russell Sq WC1	30	C3
Russell St WC2	31	D4
Rust Sq SE5	48	B4
Rutherford St SW1	46	B1
Rutland Gdns SW7	36	C3
Rutland Gate SW7	36	C3
Rutland Pk NW2	18	A1
Rutland St SW7	36	C4
Ryder Dr SE16	49	F2
Ryder St SW1	38	A2
Ryland Rd NW5	21	F1
Rylston Rd SW6	43	D3
Rysbrack St SW3	37	D4

S

Name	Page	Grid
Sable St N1	23	F2
Sackville St W1	38	A1
Saffron Hill EC1	31	E2
Sail St SE11	47	D1
St. Agnes Pl SE11	47	E3
St. Albans Gro W8	35	F4
St. Alban's Pl N1	23	F3
St. Andrew's Hill EC4	39	F1
St. Andrews Pl NW1	29	F2
St. Andrews Rd W14	42	C3
St. Andrew St EC4	31	E3
St. Anns Rd W11	34	B1
St. Ann's St SW1	38	B4
St. Ann's Ter NW8	20	B4
St. Anns Vil W11	34	B2
St. Anthonys Cl E1	41	E2
St. Augustines Rd NW1	22	B2
St. Barnabas St SW1	45	E2
St. Botolph St EC3	33	D4
St. Bride St EC4	31	F4
St. Chad's Pl WC1	30	C1
St. Chad's St WC1	30	C1
St. Charles Sq W10	26	C3
St. Clements St N7	23	E1
St. Cross St EC1	31	E3
St. Cuthberts Rd NW2	19	D1
St. Dunstan's Hill EC3	40	C1
St. Dunstans Rd W6	42	B2
St. Edmunds Sq SW13	42	A3
St. Edmunds Ter NW8	20	C3
St. Ervans Rd W10	26	C3
St. Georges Circ SE1	39	F4
St. George's Dr SW1	45	F1
St. Georges Flds W2	28	C4
St. Georges Rd SE1	39	E4
St. George's Sq SW1	46	B2
St. George's Sq Ms SW1	46	B2
St. George St W1	29	F4
St. Georges Way SE15	48	C3
St. George Wf SW8	46	C2
St. Giles High St WC2	30	B4
St. Giles Rd SE5	48	C4
St. Helens Gdns W10	26	B4
St. Hildas Cl NW6	18	B2
St. James's Ct SW1	38	A4
St. James's Gdns W11	34	C2
St. James's Palace SW1	38	A2
St. James's Pk SW1	38	B3
St. James's Pl SW1	38	A2
St. James's Rd SE1	49	E2
St. James's Rd SE16	41	E4
St. James's Sq SW1	38	A2
St. James's St SW1	38	A2
St. James's Ter Ms NW8	21	D3
St. James St W6	42	A2
St. James's Wk EC1	31	F2
St. John's Est N1	24	B4
St. John's Gdns W11	35	D1
St. John's La EC1	31	F2
St. John St EC1	31	F2
St. John's Wd High St NW8	20	B4
St. John's Wd Pk NW8	20	B3
St. John's Wd Rd NW8	28	B2
St. John's Wd Ter NW8	20	B4
St. Jude's Rd E2	25	F4
St. Julian's Rd NW6	19	D2
St. Katharine's Way E1	41	D2
St. Laurence Cl NW6	18	B3
St. Lawrence Ter W10	26	C3
St. Leonards Ct N1	32	B1
St. Leonards Sq NW5	21	E1
St. Leonard's Ter SW3	45	D2
St. Loo Av SW3	44	C3
St. Luke's Cl EC1	32	A2
St. Luke's Est EC1	32	B1
St. Lukes Rd W11	27	D3
St. Luke's St SW3	44	C2
St. Luke's Yd W9	19	D4
St. Margarets La W8	35	F4
St. Margaret's Rd NW10	26	A1
St. Margaret's St SW1	38	C3
St. Marks Cres NW1	21	E3
St. Mark's Gro SW10	43	F3
St. Marks Pl W11	26	C4
St. Marks Rd W10	26	B4
St. Marks Rd W11	26	C4
St. Marks Sq NW1	21	E3
St. Mark St E1	33	D4
St. Martins Cl NW1	22	A3
St. Martin's La WC2	38	C1
St. Martin's-le-Grand EC1	32	A4
St. Martin's Pl WC2	38	C1
St. Mary Abbots Pl W8	35	D4
St. Mary at Hill EC3	40	C1
St. Mary Axe EC3	32	C4
St. Mary's Gdns SE11	47	E1
St. Mary's Gate W8	35	F4
St. Mary's Gro N1	23	F1
St. Marys Mans W2	28	A3
St. Marys Path N1	23	F3
St. Mary's Pl W8	35	F4
St. Marys Sq W2	28	B3
St. Marys Ter W2	28	B3
St. Mary's Wk SE11	47	E1
St. Matthew's Row E2	33	E1
St. Michaels St W2	28	B4
St. Olaf's Rd SW6	42	C4
St. Oswald's Pl SE11	47	D2
St. Pancras Way NW1	22	A2
St. Paul's Chyd EC4	31	F4
St. Paul's Cres NW1	22	B2
St. Paul's Pl N1	24	B1
St. Paul's Rd N1	23	F1
St. Paul's Shrubbery N1	24	B1
St. Paul St N1	24	A3
St. Petersburgh Ms W2	35	F1
St. Petersburgh Pl W2	35	F1
St. Peter's Cl E2	25	E4
St. Peters St N1	23	F3
St. Peters Ter SW6	42	C4
St. Peter's Way N1	24	C2
St. Philip's Rd E8	25	E1
St. Quintin Av W10	26	A3
St. Quintin Gdns W10	26	A3

St. S-Sou

Name	Page	Grid
St. Saviour's Est SE1	41	D4
St. Silas Pl NW5	21	E1
St. Silas St Est NW5	21	E1
St. Stephens Cres W2	27	E4
St. Stephens Gdns W2	27	E4
St. Stephens Ter SW8	47	D4
St. Stephen's Wk SW7	44	A1
St. Swithin's La EC4	40	B1
St. Thomas's Sq E9	25	F2
St. Thomas St SE1	40	B2
St. Thomas's Way SW6	43	D4
Salamanca St SE1	46	C1
Salem Rd W2	35	F1
Sale Pl W2	28	C3
Salisbury Ct EC4	31	F4
Salisbury Pl SW9	47	F4
Salisbury Pl W1	29	D3
Salisbury St NW8	28	C2
Salters Rd W10	26	B2
Saltram Cres W9	27	D1
Salusbury Rd NW6	18	C3
Samford St NW8	28	C2
Sampson St E1	41	E2
Samuel Lewis Trust Dws SW6	43	E4
Samuel St SE15	49	D4
Sancroft St SE11	47	D2
Sandall Rd NW5	22	A1
Sandgate St SE15	49	F3
Sandland St WC1	31	D3
Sandwell Cres NW6	19	E1
Sandwich St WC1	30	C1
Sandy's Row E1	32	C3
Sansom St SE5	48	B4
Sans Wk EC1	31	E2
Saperton Wk SE11	47	D1
Satchwell Rd E2	33	E1
Saunders St SE11	47	E1
Savile Row W1	38	A1
Savona Est SW8	46	A4
Savona St SW8	46	A4
Savoy Pl WC2	38	C1
Savoy St WC2	39	D1
Sawyer St SE1	40	A3
Scala St W1	30	A3
Scampston Ms W10	26	B4
Scandrett St E1	41	F2
Scarsdale Vil W8	35	E4
Scawfell St E2	25	D4
Sclater St E1	33	D2
Scoresby St SE1	39	F2
Scott Ellis Gdns NW8	28	B1
Scott Lidgett Cres SE16	41	E3
Scott St E1	33	F2
Scriven St E8	25	D3
Scrutton St EC2	32	C2
Seaford St WC1	31	D1
Seagrave Rd SW6	43	E3
Searles Cl SW11	44	C4
Searles Rd SE1	48	B1
Sears St SE5	48	B4
Sebastian St EC1	31	F1
Sebbon St N1	23	F2
Second Av W10	26	C2
Sedding St SW1	45	E1
Sedgmoor Pl SE5	48	C4
Sedlescombe Rd SW6	43	D3
Seething La EC3	40	C1
Sekforde St EC1	31	F2
Selby St E1	33	E2
Selwood Pl SW7	44	B2
Semley Pl SW1	45	E1
Senior St W2	27	F3
Serle St WC2	31	D4
Serpentine Rd W2	37	D2
Settles St E1	33	E3
Seville Ms N1	24	C2
Seville St SW1	37	D3
Sevington St W9	27	F2
Seward St EC1	32	A1
Seymour Ms W1	29	E4
Seymour Pl W1	28	C3
Seymour St W1	29	D4
Seymour St W1	29	D4
Seymour Wk SW10	44	A3
Shacklewell St E2	33	D2
Shad Thames SE1	41	D2
Shaftesbury Av W1	38	B1
Shaftesbury Av WC2	38	B1
Shaftesbury St N1	24	A4
Shalcomb St SW10	44	A3
Shalfleet Dr W10	34	B1
Shand St SE1	40	C3
Sharplesshall St NW1	21	E4
Sharsted St SE17	47	F2
Shawfield St SW3	44	C2
Shearling Way N7	22	C1
Sheep La E8	25	F3
Sheffield Ter W8	35	E2
Sheldon Sq W2	28	A3
Sheldrake Pl W8	35	D3
Shelton St WC2	30	C4
Shenfield St N1	24	C4
Shepherdess Wk N1	24	A4
Shepherds Bush Grn W12	34	A3
Shepherds Bush Mkt W12	34	A3
Shepherds Bush Pl W12	34	B3
Shepherds Bush Rd W6	42	A1
Sheppard Dr SE16	49	F2
Shepperton Rd N1	24	A3
Sherborne St N1	24	B3
Sherbrooke Rd SW6	43	D4
Sheringham Rd N7	23	D1
Sherriff Rd NW6	19	E1
Sherwood Gdns SE16	49	E2
Shinfield St W12	26	A4
Shipton St E2	33	D1
Shirland Ms W9	27	D1
Shirland Rd W9	27	E1
Shoe La EC4	31	E4
Shoreditch High St E1	32	C2
Shorncliffe Rd SE1	49	D2
Shorrolds Rd SW6	43	D4
Shorter St E1	41	D1
Shortlands W6	42	B1
Shorts Gdns WC2	30	C4
Shouldham St W1	28	C3
Shrewsbury Rd W2	27	E4
Shrewsbury St W10	26	A2
Shroton St NW1	28	C3
Shrubland Rd E8	25	E3
Sidmouth Rd NW2	18	A2
Sidmouth St WC1	30	C1
Sidney St E1	33	F3
Sidworth St E8	25	F2
Silchester Rd W10	26	B4
Silex St SE1	39	F3
Silk St EC2	32	A3
Silver Rd W12	34	B1
Silverton Rd W6	42	B3
Simms Rd SE1	49	E1
Sinclair Gdns W14	34	B3
Sinclair St W14	34	B3
Sirdar Rd W11	34	B1
Sirinham Pt SW8	47	D3
Sivill Ho E2	33	D1
Six Bridges Trd Est SE1	49	E2
Sixth Av W10	26	C1
Skelwith Rd W6	42	A3
Skinner St EC1	31	E1
Slaidburn St SW10	44	A3
Sleaford St SW8	46	A4
Slippers Pl SE16	41	F4
Sloane Av SW3	44	C1
Sloane Ct W SW3	45	E2
Sloane Gdns SW1	45	E1
Sloane Sq SW1	45	D1
Sloane St SW1	37	D3
Sloane Ter SW1	45	D1
Smeaton St E1	41	F2
Smith Sq SW1	38	C4
Smith St SW3	45	D2
Smith Ter SW3	45	D2
Smokehouse Yd EC1	31	F3
Smyrks Rd SE17	48	C2
Smyrna Rd NW6	19	E2
Snarsgate St W10	26	A3
Snowden St EC2	32	C2
Snow Hill EC1	31	F3
Snowman Ho NW6	19	F3
Snowsfields SE1	40	B3
Soho Sq W1	30	B4
Somerford St E1	33	F2
Somers Cres W2	28	C4
Somerset Sq W14	34	C3
Sondes St SE17	48	B3
Sopwith Way SW8	45	F4
Sotheran Cl E8	25	E3
Sotheron Rd SW6	43	F4
Souldern Rd W14	34	B4
Southall Pl SE1	40	B3
Southampton Pl WC1	30	C3
Southampton Row WC1	30	C3
Southampton St WC2	38	C1
Southampton Way SE5	48	B4
Southam St W10	26	C2
South Audley St W1	37	E1
Southbank Business Cen SW8	46	B3
South Bolton Gdns SW5	43	F2
South Carriage Dr SW1	36	C3
South Carriage Dr SW7	36	C3
Southcombe St W14	42	C1
South Cres WC1	30	B3
South Eaton Pl SW1	45	E1
South Edwardes Sq W8	35	D4
South End Row W8	35	F4
Southern Row W10	26	C2
Southern St N1	23	D4
Southerton Rd W6	34	A4
Southgate Gro N1	24	B2
Southgate Rd N1	24	B3
South Island Pl SW9	47	D4
South Lambeth Pl SW8	46	C3
South Lambeth Rd SW8	46	C3
South Molton La W1	29	F4
South Molton St W1	29	F4
South Par SW3	44	B2
South Pl EC2	32	B3
South St W1	37	E2
South Tenter St E1	41	D1
South Ter SW7	44	C1
South Vil NW1	22	B1
Southwark Br EC4	40	A2
Southwark Br SE1	40	A2
Southwark Br Rd SE1	39	F4
Southwark Pk Est SE16	49	F1
Southwark Pk Rd SE16	49	D1
Southwark St SE1	39	F2
Southwell Gdns SW7	44	A1
South Wf Rd W2	28	B4

Street	Page	Grid
Southwick Pl W2	28	C4
Southwick St W2	28	C4
Sovereign Cl E1	41	F1
Spa Grn Est EC1	31	E1
Spanish Pl W1	29	E4
Spa Rd SE16	41	D4
Spear Ms SW5	43	E1
Speke Ho SE5	48	A4
Spelman St E1	33	E3
Spencer St EC1	31	F1
Spenser St SW1	38	A4
Spital Sq E1	32	C3
Spital St E1	33	E2
Sprimont Pl SW3	45	D2
Springall St SE15	49	F4
Springfield La NW6	19	F3
Springfield Rd NW8	20	A3
Springfield Wk NW6	19	F3
Spring St W2	28	B4
Springvale Ter W14	34	B4
Spurgeon St SE1	40	B4
Spur Rd SE1	39	E3
Spur Rd SW1	38	A3
Square, The W6	42	A2
Squirries St E2	33	E1
Stables Way SE11	47	E2
Stable Yd Rd SW1	38	A2
Stacey St WC2	30	B4
Stadium St SW10	44	A4
Stafford Cl NW6	27	E1
Stafford Ct W8	35	E4
Stafford Pl SW1	38	A4
Stafford Rd NW6	27	E1
Stafford St W1	38	A2
Stafford Ter W8	35	E4
Stag Pl SW1	38	A4
Stainer St SE1	40	B2
Staining La EC2	32	A4
Stalham St SE16	41	F4
Stamford Rd N1	24	C2
Stamford St SE1	39	E2
Stamp Pl E2	33	D1
Stanford Rd W8	35	F4
Stanhope Gdns SW7	44	A1
Stanhope Gate W1	37	E2
Stanhope Ms E SW7	44	A1
Stanhope Ms W SW7	44	A1
Stanhope Pl W2	29	D4
Stanhope St NW1	30	A1
Stanhope Ter W2	36	B1
Stanlake Ms W12	34	A2
Stanley Cl SW8	47	D3
Stanley Cres W11	35	D1
Stanley Gdns W11	35	D1
Stannard Ms E8	25	E1
Stannard Rd E8	25	E1
Stannary Pl SE11	47	E2
Stannary St SE11	47	E3
Stanswood Gdns SE5	48	C4
Stanway St N1	24	C4
Stanwick Rd W14	43	D1
Stanworth St SE1	41	D3
Staple Inn Bldgs WC1	31	E3
Staple St SE1	40	B3
Starcross St NW1	30	A1
Star Rd W14	43	D3
Star St W2	28	C3
Station App SE1	39	E3
Station Par NW2	18	A1
Station Ter NW10	18	B4
Staverton Rd NW2	18	A2
Stead St SE17	48	B1
Stean St E8	25	D3
Stebbing Ho W11	34	B2
Steeles Rd NW3	21	D1
Stephan Cl E8	25	E3
Stephenson Way NW1	30	A2
Stephen St W1	30	B3
Stepney Way E1	33	F3
Sterndale Rd W14	34	B4
Sterne St W12	34	B3
Sterry St SE1	40	B3
Stevenage Rd SW6	42	B4
Stevenson Cres SE16	49	E2
Steward St E1	32	C3
Stewart's Gro SW3	44	B1
Stewart's Rd SW8	46	A1
Stillington St SW1	46	A1
Stockholm Ho E1	41	E1
Stockholm Way E1	41	E2
Stone Bldgs WC2	31	D3
Stonecutter St EC4	31	F4
Stonefield St N1	23	E3
Stoneleigh Pl W11	34	B1
Stoneleigh St W11	34	B1
Stones End St SE1	40	A3
Stoney St SE1	40	B2
Stonor Rd W14	43	D1
Stopes St SE15	49	D4
Stopford Rd SE17	47	F2
Store St WC1	30	B3
Storey's Gate SW1	38	B3
Storks Rd SE16	41	E4
Stourcliffe St W1	29	D4
Strand WC2	38	C1
Stranraer Way N1	22	C2
Stratford Pl W1	29	F4
Stratford Rd W8	35	E4
Stratford Vil NW1	22	A2
Strathearn Pl W2	36	C1
Strathnairn St SE1	49	E1
Strathray Gdns NW3	20	C1
Stratton St W1	37	F2
Streatham St WC1	30	B4
Streatley Rd NW6	19	D2
Strode Rd SW6	42	B4
Strutton Grd SW1	38	B4
Stuart Rd NW6	27	E1
Stuart Twr W9	28	A1
Stubbs Dr SE16	49	F2
Studd St N1	23	F3
Studholme St SE15	49	F4
Stukeley St WC2	30	C4
Sturgeon Rd SE17	48	A2
Sturt St N1	24	A4
Stutfield St E1	33	E4
Sudeley St N1	23	F4
Sugar Quay Wk EC3	40	C1
Sulgrave Rd W6	34	A3
Sullivan Rd SE11	47	E1
Sultan St SE5	48	A4
Summerfield Av NW6	18	C4
Sumner Est SE15	49	D4
Sumner Pl SW7	44	B1
Sumner Rd SE15	49	D4
Sumner St SE1	40	A2
Sumpter Cl NW3	20	A1
Sunbeam Cres W10	26	A2
Sunderland Ter W2	27	F4
Sunlight Sq E2	33	F1
Sun Rd W14	43	D2
Sun St EC2	32	B3
Surma Cl E1	33	F2
Surrendale Pl W9	27	E2
Surrey Row SE1	39	F3
Surrey Sq SE17	48	C2
Surrey St WC2	39	D1
Surrey Ter SE17	48	C2
Sussex Gdns W2	28	B4
Sussex Pl NW1	29	D1
Sussex Pl W2	28	B4
Sussex Pl W6	42	A2
Sussex Sq W2	36	B1
Sussex St SW1	45	F2
Sutherland Av W9	28	A1
Sutherland Pl W2	27	E4
Sutherland Row SW1	45	F2
Sutherland Sq SE17	48	A2
Sutherland St SW1	45	F2
Sutherland Wk SE17	48	A2
Sutterton St N7	23	D1
Sutton Est SW3	44	C2
Sutton Est W10	26	A3
Sutton Est, The N1	23	F2
Sutton Row W1	30	B4
Sutton Way W10	26	A3
Swain St NW8	28	C2
Swanfield St E2	33	D1
Swan Mead SE1	40	C4
Swanscombe Rd W11	34	B2
Swan St SE1	40	A4
Swan Wk SW3	45	D3
Swedenborg Gdns E1	41	E1
Sweeney Cres SE1	41	D3
Swinbrook Rd W10	26	C3
Swinton Pl WC1	31	D1
Swinton St WC1	31	D1
Swiss Ter NW6	20	B2
Sydney Cl SW3	44	B1
Sydney Ms SW3	44	B1
Sydney Pl SW7	44	B1
Sydney St SW3	44	C1
Sylvan Gro SE15	49	F4
Sylvester Rd E8	25	F1
Symons St SW3	45	D1

T

Street	Page	Grid
Tabard Gdn Est SE1	40	B3
Tabard St SE1	40	B3
Tabernacle St EC2	32	B2
Tachbrook Est SW1	46	B2
Tachbrook St SW1	46	A1
Tadema Rd SW10	44	A4
Tadmor St W12	34	B2
Talacre Rd NW5	21	E1
Talbot Rd W2	27	D4
Talbot Rd W11	27	D4
Talbot Sq W2	28	B4
Talbot Wk W11	26	C4
Talgarth Rd W6	42	C2
Talgarth Rd W14	42	C2
Tallis St EC4	39	E1
Tamworth St SW6	43	E3
Tanner St SE1	40	C3
Taplow NW3	20	B2
Taplow St N1	24	A4
Tapp St E1	33	F2
Tarling St E1	33	F4
Tarrant Pl W1	29	D3
Tarver Rd SE17	47	F2
Tasso Rd W6	42	C3
Tatum St SE17	48	B1
Taunton Pl NW1	29	D2
Tavistock Cres W11	27	D3
Tavistock Pl WC1	30	C2
Tavistock Rd W11	27	D4
Tavistock Sq WC1	30	B2
Tavistock St WC2	38	C1
Taviton St WC1	30	B2
Tavy Cl SE11	47	E2
Tayport Cl N1	22	C2

Tea-Vau 73

Name	Page	Grid
Teale St E2	25	E4
Tedworth Sq SW3	45	D2
Teesdale Cl E2	25	F4
Teesdale St E2	25	F4
Telford Rd W10	26	C3
Telford Ter SW1	46	A3
Temple, The EC4	39	E1
Temple Av EC4	39	E1
Temple Pl WC2	39	D1
Temple St E2	25	F4
Templeton Pl SW5	43	E1
Temple W Ms SE11	39	F4
Tench St E1	41	F2
Tenison Way SE1	39	D2
Tennis St SE1	40	B3
Tennyson Rd NW6	19	D3
Tenterden St W1	29	F4
Tent St E1	33	F2
Terminus Pl SW1	37	F4
Terrace, The NW6	19	E3
Testerton Wk W11	34	B1
Tetcott Rd SW10	44	A4
Thackeray St W8	35	F3
Thanet St WC1	30	C1
Thaxton Rd W14	43	D3
Thayer St W1	29	E3
Theberton St N1	23	E3
Theed St SE1	39	E2
Theobald's Rd WC1	31	D3
Thessaly Rd SW8	46	A4
Third Av W10	26	C1
Thirleby Rd SW1	38	A4
Thistle Gro SW10	44	A2
Thomas Darby Ct W11	26	C4
Thomas Doyle St SE1	39	F4
Thomas More St E1	41	E1
Thompson's Av SE5	48	A4
Thorburn Sq SE1	49	E1
Thoresby St N1	32	A1
Thorncroft St SW8	46	C4
Thorndike Cl SW10	44	A4
Thorndike Rd N1	24	A1
Thorndike St SW1	46	A1
Thorne Rd SW8	46	C4
Thorney Cres SW11	44	B4
Thorney St SW1	46	C1
Thorngate Rd W9	27	E2
Thornhaugh St WC1	30	B2
Thornhill Cres N1	23	D2
Thornhill Rd N1	23	E2
Thornhill Sq N1	23	D2
Thornton Pl W1	29	D3
Thrale St SE1	40	A2
Thrawl St E1	33	D3
Threadneedle St EC2	32	B4
Three Colts La E2	33	F2
Three Kings Yd W1	37	E1
Three Quays Wk EC3	40	C1
Threshers Pl W11	34	C1
Throgmorton Av EC2	32	B4
Throgmorton St EC2	32	B4
Thurland Rd SE16	41	E4
Thurloe Cl SW7	36	C4
Thurloe Pl SW7	44	B1
Thurloe Sq SW7	44	C1
Thurloe St SW7	44	B1
Thurlow St SE17	48	B2
Thurtle Rd E2	25	D3
Tideway Ind Est SW8	46	A3
Tileyard Rd N7	22	C2
Tilney Gdns N1	24	B1
Tilney St W1	37	E2
Tilton St SW6	42	C3
Timberland Rd E1	33	F4
Tinworth St SE11	47	D2
Tisdall Pl SE17	48	B1
Titchfield Rd NW8	21	D3
Tite St SW3	45	D2
Tiverton Rd NW10	18	B3
Tiverton St SE1	40	A4
Tobacco Dock E1	41	F1
Tobin Cl NW3	20	C2
Tollgate Gdns NW6	19	F4
Tolpuddle St N1	23	E4
Tomlinson Cl E2	33	D1
Tonbridge St WC1	30	C1
Tooley St SE1	40	B2
Torbay Rd NW6	19	D2
Tor Gdns W8	35	E3
Torrens St EC1	23	E4
Torrington Pl E1	41	E2
Torrington Pl WC1	30	B3
Torrington Sq WC1	30	B2
Tothill St SW1	38	B3
Tottenham Ct Rd W1	30	A2
Tottenham Rd N1	24	C1
Tottenham St W1	30	A3
Toulmin St SE1	40	A4
Toulon St SE5	48	A4
Tournay Rd SW6	43	D4
Tower 42 EC2	32	C4
Tower Br E1	41	D2
Tower Br SE1	41	D2
Tower Br App E1	41	D2
Tower Br Rd SE1	40	C4
Tower Br Wf E1	41	E2
Tower Hill EC3	40	C1
Tower Millennium Pier EC3	41	D2
Tower St WC2	30	B4
Townsend St SE17	48	B1
Townsend Est NW8	20	C4
Townshend Rd NW8	20	C3
Toynbee St E1	33	D3
Tradescant Rd SW8	46	C4
Trafalgar Av SE15	49	D2
Trafalgar Sq SW1	38	B2
Trafalgar Sq WC2	38	B2
Trafalgar St SE17	48	B2
Transept St NW1	28	C3
Tranton Rd SE16	41	E4
Treadgold St W11	34	B1
Treadway St E2	25	F4
Treaty St N1	23	D3
Trebovir Rd SW5	43	E2
Trederwen Rd E8	25	E3
Tregunter Rd SW10	44	A3
Trellick Twr W10	27	D2
Trenchold St SW8	46	C3
Tresham Cres NW8	28	C2
Trevanion Rd W14	42	C2
Trevelyan Gdns NW10	18	A3
Treverton St W10	26	B2
Trevor Pl SW7	36	C3
Trevor Sq SW7	37	D3
Trevor St SW7	36	C3
Triangle Rd E8	25	F3
Trigon Rd SW8	47	D4
Trinity Ch Sq SE1	40	A4
Trinity Cl E8	25	D1
Trinity Sq EC3	40	C1
Trinity St SE1	40	A3
Trinity Wk NW3	20	A1
Triton Sq NW1	30	A2
Trocadero Shop Cen W1	38	B1
Truro St NW5	21	E1
Trussley Rd W6	34	A4
Tryon St SW3	45	D2
Tudor Rd E9	25	F3
Tudor St EC4	39	E1
Tufton St SW1	38	B4
Tuilerie St E2	25	E4
Turin St E2	33	E1
Turks Row SW3	45	D2
Turner St E1	33	F3
Turneville Rd W14	43	D3
Turnmill St EC1	31	E2
Turnpike Ho EC1	31	F1
Twyford St N1	23	D3
Tyburn Way W1	37	D1
Tyers Est SE1	40	C3
Tyers St SE11	47	D2
Tyers Ter SE11	47	D2
Tyler Cl E2	25	D4
Tyssen Pas E8	25	D1
Tyssen St E8	25	D1

U

Name	Page	Grid
Ufford St SE1	39	E3
Ufton Gro N1	24	B2
Ufton Rd N1	24	B2
Undershaft EC3	32	C4
Underwood Rd E1	33	E2
Underwood Row N1	32	A1
Underwood St N1	32	A1
Union Sq N1	24	A3
Union St SE1	39	F2
University St WC1	30	A2
Unwin Cl SE15	49	E3
Upcerne Rd SW10	44	A4
Upper Addison Gdns W14	34	C3
Upper Belgrave St SW1	37	E4
Upper Berkeley St W1	29	D4
Upper Brook St W1	37	E1
Upper Cheyne Row SW3	44	C3
Upper Grosvenor St W1	37	E1
Upper Grd SE1	39	E2
Upper Marsh SE1	39	D4
Upper Montagu St W1	29	D3
Upper Phillimore Gdns W8	35	E3
Upper St N1	23	E4
Upper Tachbrook St SW1	46	A1
Upper Thames St EC4	40	A1
Upper Wimpole St W1	29	E3
Upper Woburn Pl WC1	30	B1
Urlwin St SE5	48	A3
Usborne Ms SW8	47	D4
Uverdale Rd SW10	44	A4
Uxbridge St W8	35	E2

V

Name	Page	Grid
Vale, The SW3	44	B3
Valentine Pl SE1	39	F3
Valentine Row SE1	39	F3
Vale Royal N7	22	C2
Valette St E9	25	F1
Vallance Rd E1	33	E2
Vallance Rd E2	33	E1
Vandon St SW1	38	A4
Vanston Pl SW6	43	E4
Varcoe Rd SE16	49	E1
Varden St E1	33	F4
Varna Rd SW6	42	C4
Varndell St NW1	30	A1
Vassall Rd SW9	47	E4
Vauban Est SE16	41	E4
Vauban St SE16	41	D4
Vaughan Way E1	41	E1

74 Vau-Wes

Name	Page	Grid
Vauxhall Br SE1	46	C2
Vauxhall Br SE1	46	C2
Vauxhall Br Rd SW1	46	A1
Vauxhall Gdns Est SE11	47	D2
Vauxhall Gro SW8	46	C3
Vauxhall St SE11	47	D2
Vauxhall Wk SE11	47	D2
Venables St NW8	28	B2
Vereker Rd W14	42	C2
Vere St W1	29	F4
Verity Cl W11	26	C4
Verney Rd SE16	49	E3
Verney Way SE16	49	F2
Vernon Pl WC1	30	C3
Vernon Ri WC1	31	D1
Vernon St W14	42	C1
Vestry St N1	32	B1
Viaduct St E2	33	F1
Vicarage Gdns W8	35	E2
Vicarage Gate W8	35	F3
Victoria Embk EC4	39	D1
Victoria Embk SW1	38	C3
Victoria Embk WC2	38	C3
Victoria Gdns W11	35	E2
Victoria Gro W8	36	A4
Victoria Ms NW6	19	E3
Victoria Pl SW1	45	F1
Victoria Rd NW6	19	D3
Victoria Rd W8	36	A4
Victoria Sta SW1	45	F1
Victoria St SW1	38	A4
Victory Pl SE17	48	A1
Vigo St W1	38	A1
Viking Ct SW6	43	E3
Villa St SE17	48	B2
Villiers St WC2	38	C1
Vincent Sq SW1	46	A1
Vincent St SW1	46	B1
Vincent Ter N1	23	F4
Vince St EC1	32	B1
Vine Sq W14	43	D2
Vine St Br EC1	31	E2
Vineyard Wk EC1	31	E2
Violet Hill NW8	20	A4
Virgil St SE1	39	D4
Virginia Rd E2	33	D1
Virginia St E1	41	E1
Voss St E2	33	E1
Vulcan Way N7	23	D1
Vyner St E2	25	F3

W

Name	Page	Grid
Wadding St SE17	48	B1
Wadeson St E2	25	F4
Wadham Gdns NW3	20	C3
Waite St SE15	49	D3
Wakefield St WC1	30	C1
Wakeham St N1	24	B1
Wakeman Rd NW10	26	A1
Wakley St EC1	31	F1
Walberswick St SW8	46	C4
Walbrook EC4	40	B1
Walcot Sq SE11	47	E1
Walden St E1	33	F4
Wales Cl SE15	49	F4
Walham Gro SW6	43	E4
Wallace Rd N1	24	A1
Wallgrave Rd SW5	43	F1
Wallingford Av W10	26	B3
Wall St N1	24	B1
Walmer Rd W11	34	C1
Walnut Tree Wk SE11	47	E1
Walpole St SW3	45	D2
Walterton Rd W9	27	D2
Walton Cl SW8	46	C4
Walton Pl SW3	37	D4
Walton St SW3	44	C1
Walworth Pl SE17	48	A2
Walworth Rd SE1	48	A1
Walworth Rd SE17	48	A1
Wandon Rd SW6	43	F4
Wansey St SE17	48	A1
Wapping High St E1	41	E1
Wapping La E1	41	F1
Warburton Rd E8	25	F2
Warden Rd NW5	21	E1
Wardour St W1	38	B1
Warfield Rd NW10	26	B1
Warham St SE5	47	F4
Warlock Rd W9	27	E2
Warneford St E9	25	F3
Warner Pl E2	25	E4
Warner St EC1	31	E2
Warren St W1	30	A2
Warrington Cres W9	28	A2
Warwick Av W2	28	A2
Warwick Av W9	28	A2
Warwick Cres W2	28	A3
Warwick Est W2	27	F3
Warwick Gdns W14	35	D4
Warwick Ho St SW1	38	B2
Warwick La EC4	31	F4
Warwick Pl W9	28	A3
Warwick Pl N SW1	46	A1
Warwick Rd SW5	43	D1
Warwick Rd W14	43	D1
Warwick Row SW1	37	F4
Warwick Sq SW1	46	A2
Warwick Sq Ms SW1	46	A1
Warwick St W1	38	A1
Warwick Way SW1	46	A1
Water Gdns, The W2	28	C4
Waterloo Br SE1	39	D1
Waterloo Br WC2	39	D1
Waterloo Pas NW6	19	D2
Waterloo Pl SW1	38	B2
Waterloo Rd SE1	39	E3
Waterloo Ter N1	23	F2
Waterman Way E1	41	F2
Waterside Pt SW11	44	C4
Waterson St E2	32	C1
Watkinson Rd N7	23	D1
Watling Gdns NW2	18	C1
Watling St EC4	32	A4
Watney St E1	33	F4
Watts St E1	41	F2
Waverley Pl NW8	20	B4
Waverley Wk W2	27	E3
Waverton St W1	37	E2
Wayman Ct E8	25	F1
Waynflete Sq W10	34	B1
Wear Pl E2	33	F1
Weavers Ter SW6	43	E3
Weaver St E1	33	E2
Weavers Way NW1	22	B3
Webb Cl W10	26	A2
Webber Row SE1	39	F3
Webber St SE1	39	E3
Webb St SE1	40	C4
Webheath Est NW6	19	D2
Webster Rd SE16	41	E4
Weighhouse St W1	29	E4
Weir's Pas NW1	30	B1
Welbeck St W1	29	E3
Welbeck Way W1	29	F4
Wellclose Sq E1	41	E1
Wellesley Ter N1	32	A1
Wellington Pl NW8	20	C4
Wellington Rd NW8	20	B4
Wellington Rd NW10	26	B1
Wellington Row E2	33	D1
Wellington Sq SW3	45	D2
Wellington St WC2	38	C1
Wellington Ter E1	41	F2
Wells Ri NW8	21	D3
Wells Rd W12	34	A3
Wells St W1	30	A4
Well St E9	25	F2
Wells Way SE5	48	B3
Wells Way SW7	36	B4
Welsford St SE1	49	E2
Wendle Ct SW8	46	C3
Wendover St E17	48	C2
Wenlock Rd N1	24	A4
Wenlock St N1	24	A4
Wentworth Cres SE15	49	E4
Wentworth St E1	33	D4
Werrington St NW1	22	A4
Wesley Cl SE17	47	F1
Westbourne Br W2	28	A3
Westbourne Cres W2	36	B1
Westbourne Gdns W2	27	F4
Westbourne Gro W2	27	E4
Westbourne Gro W11	35	D1
Westbourne Gro Ter W2	27	F4
Westbourne Pk Rd W2	27	E3
Westbourne Pk Rd W11	26	C4
Westbourne Pk Vil W2	27	E3
Westbourne Rd N7	23	E1
Westbourne St W2	36	B1
Westbourne Ter W2	28	B4
Westbourne Ter Ms W2	28	A4
Westbourne Ter Rd W2	28	A3
West Carriage Dr W2	36	B1
Westcott Rd SE17	47	F3
West Cromwell Rd SW5	43	D1
West Cromwell Rd W14	43	D1
West Cross Route W10	34	B1
West Cross Route W11	34	B1
West Eaton Pl SW1	45	E1
West End La NW6	19	E2
Westfield Cl SW10	44	A4
West Gdns E1	41	F1
Westgate St E8	25	F3
Westgate Ter SW10	43	F2
West Halkin St SW1	37	E4
West Hampstead Ms NW6	19	F1
West La SE16	41	F3
Westminster Br SE1	38	C3
Westminster Br SW1	38	C3
Westminster Br Rd SE1	39	E4
Westminster Gdns SW1	46	B1
Westmoreland Pl SW1	45	F2
Westmoreland Rd SE17	48	A3
Westmoreland St W1	29	E3
Westmoreland Ter SW1	45	F2
Westmoreland Wk SE17	48	B3
West One Shop Cen W1	29	F4
Weston Ri WC1	23	D4
Weston St SE1	40	B4
West Rd SW3	45	D3
West Row W10	26	C2
West Smithfield EC1	31	F3
West Sq SE11	39	F4
West St E2	25	F4
West Tenter St E1	33	D4
Westview Cl W10	26	A4
Westway W2	27	E3
Westway W9	27	E3

Wes-You

Name	Page	Grid
Westway W10	26	C4
Westwick Gdns W14	34	B3
Wetherby Gdns SW5	44	A1
Wetherby Pl SW7	44	A1
Weymouth Ms W1	29	F3
Weymouth St W1	29	F3
Weymouth Ter E2	25	D4
Wharfdale Rd N1	22	C4
Wharfedale St SW10	43	F2
Wharf Pl E2	25	E3
Wharf Rd N1	24	A4
Wharton St WC1	31	D1
Wheatsheaf La SW6	42	A4
Wheatsheaf La SW8	46	C4
Wheatsheaf Ter SW6	43	D4
Wheatstone Rd W10	26	C3
Wheelwright St N7	23	D2
Wheler St E1	33	D2
Whidborne St WC1	30	C1
Whiskin St EC1	31	F1
Whistlers Av SW11	44	B4
Whiston Rd E2	25	D4
Whitchurch Rd W11	34	B1
Whitcomb St WC2	38	B1
Whitechapel High St E1	33	D4
Whitechapel Rd E1	33	E4
White Ch La E1	33	E4
White City Cl W12	34	A1
Whitecross St EC1	32	A2
Whitefriars St EC4	31	E4
Whitehall SW1	38	C2
Whitehall Ct SW1	38	C2
Whitehall Pl SW1	38	C2
White Hart St SE11	47	E2
Whitehead's Gro SW3	44	C2
White Horse St W1	37	F2
Whiteleys Shop Cen W2	27	F4
White Lion Hill EC4	39	F1
White Lion St N1	23	E4
Whites Grds SE1	40	C3
White's Row E1	33	D3
Whitfield St W1	30	B3
Whitgift St SE11	47	D1
Whitmore Est N1	24	C3
Whitmore Gdns NW10	18	A4
Whitmore Rd N1	24	C3
Whitstable Ho W10	26	B4
Whittaker St SW1	45	E1
Wickham St SE11	47	D2
Wicklow St WC1	31	D1
Widley Rd W9	27	E1
Wigmore Pl W1	29	F4
Wigmore St W1	29	E4
Wilbraham Pl SW1	45	D1
Wilby Ms W11	35	D2
Wilcox Cl SW8	46	C4
Wilcox Rd SW8	46	C4
Wild Ct WC2	31	D4
Wilde Cl E8	25	E3
Wild's Rents SE1	40	C4
Wild St WC2	30	C4
Wilfred St SW1	38	A4
Wilkes St E1	33	D3
Wilkinson St SW8	47	D4
Wilkin St NW5	21	F1
Willesden La NW2	18	B1
Willesden La NW6	18	B1
Willes Rd NW5	21	F1
William Dunbar Ho NW6	19	D4
William IV St WC2	38	C1
William Rd NW1	29	F1
William Saville Ho NW6	19	D4
William St SW1	37	D3
Willow Br Rd N1	24	A1
Willowbrook Rd SE15	49	D3
Willow Pl SW1	46	A1
Willow St EC2	32	C2
Willow Wk SE1	48	C1
Wilman Gro E8	25	E2
Wilmcote Ho W2	27	F3
Wilmer Gdns N1	24	C3
Wilmington Sq WC1	31	E1
Wilmington St WC1	31	E1
Wilmot Cl SE15	49	E4
Wilmot Pl NW1	22	A4
Wilmot St E2	33	F2
Wilsham St W11	34	B2
Wilson Gro SE16	41	F3
Wilsons Rd W6	42	B2
Wilson St EC2	32	B3
Wilton Cres SW1	37	E3
Wilton Ms SW1	37	E4
Wilton Pl SW1	37	E3
Wilton Rd SW1	37	F4
Wilton Row SW1	37	E3
Wilton Sq N1	24	B3
Wilton St SW1	37	F4
Wilton Ter SW1	37	E4
Wilton Vil N1	24	B3
Wilton Way E8	25	E1
Wiltshire Row N1	24	B3
Wimbolt St E2	33	E1
Wimbourne St N1	24	B4
Wimpole Ms W1	29	F3
Wimpole St W1	29	F4
Winchendon Rd SW6	43	D4
Winchester Av NW6	18	C3
Winchester Cl SE17	47	F1
Winchester Rd NW3	20	B2
Winchester Sq SE1	40	B2
Winchester St SW1	45	F2
Winchester Wk SE1	40	B2
Wincott St SE11	47	E1
Windermere Av NW6	18	C3
Windmill Ct NW2	18	C1
Windmill Row SE11	47	E2
Windmill St W1	30	B3
Windmill Wk SE1	39	E2
Windsor Gdns W9	27	E3
Windsor St N1	23	F3
Windsor Ter N1	32	A1
Windsor Way W14	42	B1
Wingrave Rd W6	42	A3
Winkley St E2	25	F4
Winsland St W2	28	B4
Winsley St W1	30	A4
Winslow SE17	48	C2
Winslow Rd W6	42	A3
Winterton Ho E1	33	F4
Winthrop St E1	33	F3
Witan St E2	33	F1
Woburn Pl WC1	30	B2
Woburn Sq WC1	30	B2
Woburn Wk WC1	30	B1
Wolseley St SE1	41	D3
Wolsey Ms NW5	22	A1
Wolverton Gdns W6	42	B1
Woodbridge St EC1	31	F2
Woodchester Sq W2	27	F3
Woodchurch Rd NW6	19	E2
Wood Cl E2	33	E2
Woodfall St SW3	45	D2
Woodfield Pl W9	27	D2
Woodfield Rd W9	27	D3
Wood La W12	26	A4
Woodlawn Rd SW6	42	B4
Woodseer St E1	33	D3
Woodsford Sq W14	34	C3
Woods Ms W1	37	D1
Woodstock Gro W12	34	B3
Wood St EC2	32	A4
Woodville Rd NW6	19	D4
Wooler St SE17	48	B2
Woolstaplers Way SE16	49	E1
Wootton St SE1	39	E2
Worfield St SW11	44	C4
Worgan St SE11	47	D2
World's End Est SW10	44	B4
Worlidge St W6	42	A2
Wormwood St EC2	32	C4
Wornington Rd W10	26	C3
Woronzow Rd NW8	20	B3
Worship St EC2	32	C2
Wren St WC1	31	D2
Wrentham Av NW10	18	B4
Wrights La W8	35	F3
Wyatt Dr SW13	42	A4
Wyfold Rd SW6	42	C4
Wymering Rd W9	27	E1
Wyndham Est SE5	48	A4
Wyndham Pl W1	29	D3
Wyndham Rd SE5	47	F4
Wyndham St W1	29	D3
Wynford Rd N1	23	D4
Wynnstay Gdns W8	35	E4
Wynyard Ter SE11	47	D2
Wyvil Rd SW8	46	C3

Y

Name	Page	Grid
Yalding Rd SE16	41	E4
Yardley St WC1	31	E1
Yates Ct NW2	18	B1
Yeate St N1	24	B2
Yeldham Rd W6	42	B2
Yeoman's Row SW3	36	C4
York Br NW1	29	E2
York Gate NW1	29	E2
York Ho Pl W8	35	F3
York Rd SE1	39	D3
York St W1	29	D3
York Ter E NW1	29	E2
York Ter W NW1	29	E2
Yorkton St E2	25	E4
York Way N1	22	C3
York Way N7	22	B1
York Way Ct N1	22	C3
Young St W8	35	F3

Croydon

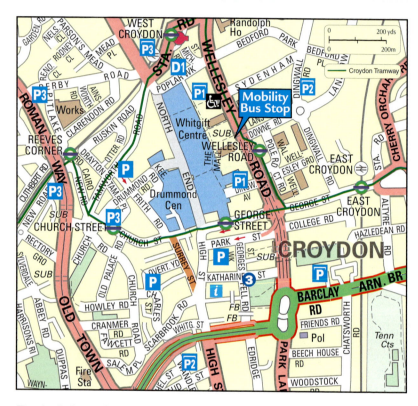

Tourist Information Centre

Information on accommodation, places to visit and transport ticket sales.

Tel: **020 8253 1009** Email: **tic@croydon.gov.uk**
www.croydon.gov.uk

Other useful sites include: **www.croydononline.org; www.visitcroydon.com**

Parking Enquiries

Tel: **020 8407 6907**
Email: **parking@croydon.gov.uk**

Address

PO Box 1462, Croydon, CR9 1WX

Greenwich

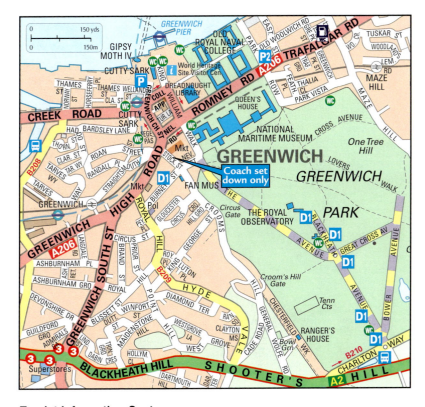

Tourist Information Centre

Information, accommodation, attractions and transport tickets.

Tel: **0870 608 2000** Email: **tic@greenwich.gov.uk**
www.greewich.gov.uk

Other useful sites include: **www.greenwichwhs.org.uk**

Parking Enquiries

Tel: **020 8921 4339**
Email: **parking@greenwich.gov.uk**

Address

2nd Floor, Poggy Middleton House, 50 Woolwich New Road,
Woolwich, London. SE18 6HQ

Kingston upon Thames

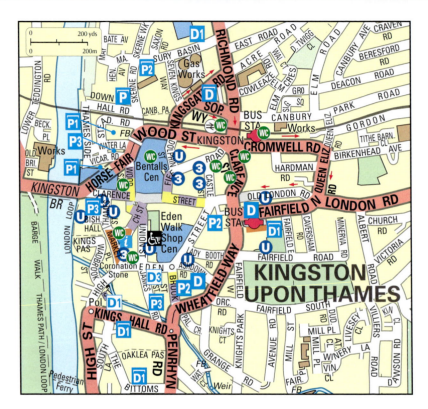

Tourist Information Centre

Local and council information services, including bus passes and National Express agents.

Tel: **020 8547 5592** E-mail: **tourist.information@rbk.kingston.gov.uk**
www.kingston.gov.uk

Other useful sites include: **www.kingstonguardian.co.uk**

Parking Enquiries

General Enquiries Tel: **020 8547 5911** Car Parks Tel: **020 8547 6156**
E-mail: **parking.schemes@rbk.kingston.gov.uk**

Address

Directorate of Environmental Services, Guildhall
Kingston upon Thames, KT1 1EU

Shopmobility

National Federation of Shopmobility UK
Tel: **08456 442 446**
Email: **info@shopmobility.co.uk**
www.justmobility.co.uk/shop

Shopmobility is a scheme which lends wheelchairs, powered wheelchairs and scooters to members of the public with limited mobility to enable them to shop and to visit leisure and commercial facilities within the town, city or shopping centre. Each Shopmobility centre varies so it is important to contact them in advance to find out what assistance is available. The name, location and contact details for the Shopmobility centres in and around London are:

Scheme Location	Contact Number	Address	Town/County	Postcode
Barking & Dagenham	020 8252 5340	51, Ripple Road	Essex	IG11 7NT
Bexley Heath	020 8301 5237	Broadway Shopping Centre	Bexley Heath	DA6 7JN
Brent Cross	020 8457 4070	Brent Cross Shopping Centre	London	NW4 3FP
Bromley	020 8313 0031	The Glades Shopping Centre Car Park	Bromley	BR1 1DN
Camden*	020 7482 5503	29a, Pratt Street, Camden	London	NW1 0BG
Croydon*	020 8688 7336	Whitgift Car Park	Croydon	CR0 2AG
Enfield	020 8366 8081	29, Genotin Road	Middlesex	EN1 2AG
Gravesend	01474 337 600	Towncentric, 18a St Georges Centre	Kent	DA11 0ZB
Harrow	020 8427 1200	37, St Georges Centre	Harrow	HA1 1HS
Hillingdon	01895 271 510	Chimes Shopping Centre	Uxbridge	UB8 1GD
Hounslow	020 8570 3343	Treaty Centre, High Street	Hounslow	TW3 1ES
Ilford (Redbridge Shopmobility)	020 8478 6864	The Exchange Mall	Ilford	IG1 1RS
Kingston*	020 8547 1255	Eden Walk Car Park	Kingston upon Thames	KT1 1BL
Lewisham	020 8297 2735	29, Molesworth Street	London	SE13 7HF
Romford (Havering Shopmobility)	01708 722 570	The Brewery	Romford	RM1 1AU
Staines	01784 459 416	Two Rivers Retail Park	Staines	TW18 4WB
Waltham Forest	020 8520 3366	Selborne Walk	London	E17 7JR
Wandsworth	020 8875 9585	45, Garratt Lane	London	SW18 4AD

* Shopmobility centres located on main map or city blow up page views

For a full list of all the Shopmobility centres in the UK visit the website or email for a booklet. This publication will be available at most Shopmobility centres.

Visit **www.justmobility.co.uk/shop** or call **08456 442 446**

Blue Badge parking concessions by Councils across London

NOTES Always check local restrictions displayed on signs, pay & display machines and street markings **Councils**	**Blue Badge** Park FREE with no time restrictions	**Pay & Display** Park FREE with no time restrictions during the enforced time period
Barking and Dagenham	✔	✔
Barnet	✔	✔
Bexley	✔	✔
Brent	✔	✔
Bromley	✔	✔
Camden (Green Badge Area)	✔	✘
Camden (Not Green Badge Area)	✔	✔
Corporation of London	✔ max stay 3hrs Mon to Fri	✘
Croydon	✔	✔
Ealing	✔	✔ 3 hrs
Enfield	✔	✔
Greenwich	✔	✔
Hackney	✔	✔
Hammersmith & Fulham	✔	✔
Haringey	✔	✔
Harrow	✔	✔
Havering	✔	✔
Hillingdon	✔	✔
Hounslow	✔ max stay 3hrs	✔
Islington	✔	✔
Kensington and Chelsea	✔ max stay 4 hrs Mon to Fri	✘ 1 hr free once payment made
Royal Borough of Kingston upon Thames	✔	✔
Lambeth	✔	✔
Lewisham	✔	✔
Merton	✔	✔
Newham	✔	✔
Redbridge	✔	✔
Richmond	✔	✔
Southwark	✔	✔
Sutton	✔	✔
Tower Hamlets	✔ max stay 3 hr in some areas	✔
Waltham Forest	✔ max stay 3 hrs	✔
Wandsworth	✔	✔
Westminster	✔ max stay 4hrs Mon to Fri	✘ 1 hr free once payment made

Free parking on Single & Double Yellow lines (3hrs max) except where un/loading restrictions apply, Pay & Display, Shared Used, Residents & Blue Badge bays

Free parking in most places (single/double yellow line, Pay & Display) except Residents Parking Bays & where un/loading restrictions apply

Free parking in most places (single/double yellow line, Pay & Display) except for Residents Parking & Shared Use Bays & where un/loading restrictions apply

Shared Use Bays (Pay & Display and Resident) Park FREE with no time restrictions during the enforced time period	Resident Bays Park with no time restrictions during the enforced time period	Single & Double Yellow Lines Park for a max. 3 hrs on a Single or Double Yellow Line during the enforced time	Council Specific Contact No. For the Blue Badge Scheme
✔	✔ max stay 4 hrs	✔	020 8227 2334
✔	✔	✔	020 8359 2000
✔	✔	✔	020 8303 7777
✔	✔	✔	020 8937 4665
✔ parking in shared use bays is goverened by P&D restrictions	✘	✔	020 8461 7629
✘	✘	✘	020 7974 4646
✔	✔	✔	020 7974 4646
n/a	✘	✘	020 7332 1548
✔	✔	✔	020 8686 4433 Ex2121
✔ 3 hrs	✔	✔	020 8825 6677
✔	✔	✔	020 8379 1000
✔	✘	✔	020 8921 2388
✔	✘	✔	020 8356 8370
✔	n/a	✔	020 8753 5134
✔	✔	✔	020 8489 1865
✔	✔	✔	020 8863 5611
n/a	✔	✔	01708 432 797
✔	✔	✔	01895 250 123
✔	✘	✔	020 8583 3073
✔	✔	✔	020 7527 1358
✘	✘	✘	020 7361 3108
✔	✔	✔	020 8547 6600
✔	✔	✔	020 7926 9000
✔	✘	✔	020 8314 8129
✔	✔	✔	020 8545 4656
✔	✔	✔	020 8430 2000
✘	✘	✔	020 8708 3636
✔	✔	✔	020 8831 6096
✔	✘	✔	0870 600 6768
✔	✔	✔	020 8770 5341
✔	✘	✔	020 7364 5843
✔	✔	✔	020 8496 1659
✔	✔	✔	020 8871 7709
✘ 1 hr free once payment made	✘	✘	020 7823 4567

Free parking in Blue Badge Bays with limited concessions on Pay & Display

Free parking in Blue Badge Bays only

Users should be aware that this information may change at any time. This information was correct as of November 2004.
Compiled by PIE Enterprises Ltd © 2004. All rights reserved.

Congestion Charge for Blue Badge Holders

Blue Badge holders are eligible for a full discount on the Congestion Charge.

This is available to Blue Badge holders from throughout the European Union. After registering and making a one off payment of £10, holders of this discount are not required to pay the congestion charge when they enter the congestion charging zone.

Note that you do need to own a vehicle or drive a vehicle to register for the discount.

The discount applies to the person who is the Blue Badge Holder, not the vehicle that is being used.

Please note that you MUST register a nominated vehicle. This can be done on the day of travel. There are various nomination rules to register for long term and short term vehicles, details of which are explained on the registration form.

The form is available from Transport for London (TfL). It can be obtained in the following ways:

Download it from the web: **www.cclondon.com/downloads/DisabledPeople.pdf**

Write to: Congestion Charging, PO Box 2982, Coventry CV7 8WR

Telephone: **0845 900 1234** or from outside the UK **+44 20 7649 9122**

Text phone: **020 7649 9123**

Please note the Congestion Charge boundary is shown in the map pages with the following line style and colour.

If you need more information on the Congestion Charge you can visit **www.cclondon.com** or call **0845 900 1234.**

Other general information about the Congestion Charge.

Congestion Charge Operating Hours: 7am - 6.30pm Monday to Friday, excluding Public Holidays.

The normal daily tariff is £5 which has to be paid by no later than 10pm on the day of travel.

Traffic signs and markings on the road should make it clear exactly where the charging zone is. Below are some examples. This map has the zone marked out.

For Congestion Charge information visit **www.cclondon.com** or call **0845 900 1234**

London Airports

General Information Travelling from Airports

For security reasons the Blue Badge scheme does not operate at most airports. Help phones will be able to offer assistance to at least get you to check-in, these are typically located near Blue Badge parking bays as well as around the terminal.

Luton Airport

Free assistance is available from Special Assistance telephones for help up to the check in. There is no charge for the use of supplied wheelchairs. In the mid and long term car parks there is an intercom to call for free assistance. To guarantee space you may want to pre-book on **01582 395456** or email: **reservations@bcponline.co.uk.**

There are designated bays in the set down area outside the main terminal (max 10 mins free). The Express Car park (near the terminal) has designated bays free for 1 hour. You will need your badge at the payment desk to get the discount. Keep the clock on show in the vehicle.

Enquiries for mobility assistance call **01582 405 100** (be prepared to wait) or email **disabledfacilities@ltn.aero**

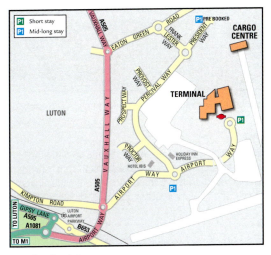

www.london-luton.com

London City Airport

www.londoncityairport.com

There are allocated disabled car parking spaces within the car park close to the terminal. There is not a lot of information from the authorities at this airport stating that they do not have many disabled visitors. However the airport and shuttle buses are all accessible.

Heathrow Airport

Heathrow general information: telephone **0870 000 0123** and textphone **020 8745 7950**

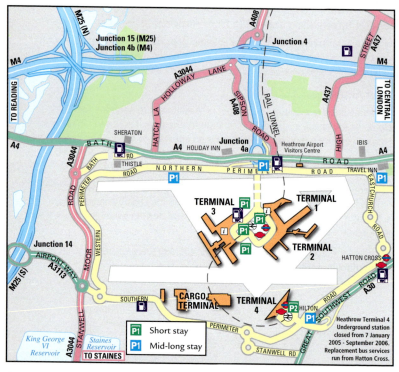

For more information, visit **www.baa.com** (look out special needs section by airport)

Help points

Free assistance is available to check-in to those with special needs. Help points are located on terminal forecourts, in short stay car parks and in bus/coach and underground stations. You may call from a Help point on site but pre-booking is better on **020 8745 6011/020 8745 5727**.

Help bus

Accessible bus operates between 06:00-23:00. Use Help bus phones or Help points on forecourts, or call directly on **020 8745 6261**.

In 1991 PIPEX was the UK's first commercial ISP

Today PIPEX is trusted by the majority of The Times Top 100 companies

Now you can trust PIPEX at home for just £15.99 a month

PIPEX professional broadband now available at home

PIPEX has been the leading choice for business for over a decade. Now you can choose it at home too. Industry leading, multi-award winning professional broadband – is it any wonder over 50% of our new customers join PIPEX through word of mouth. So if you want fast, reliable broadband that's up to 20x faster than standard dial-up at home, connect to PIPEX and get the best in broadband.

FROM JUST £15.99 A MONTH

Visit www.solo.pipex.net

Gatwick Airport

Gatwick general information: telephone **0870 000 2468** and textphone **01293 513179**

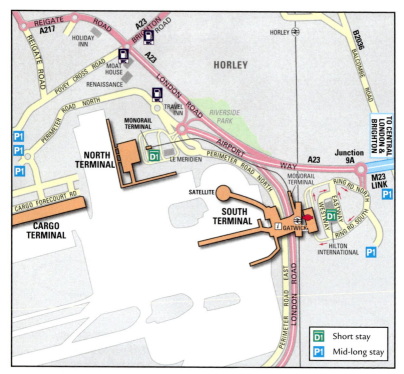

For more information, visit **www.baa.com** (look out special needs section by airport)

Help points

Help points are provided throughout the Terminals for those with Special Needs. If you require assistance to Check-in, this can be requested by picking up the Help phone at the terminal entrances, car parks or coach stations. At times there may be a wait for this service.

Stansted Airport

Stansted general information: telephone **0870 000 0303** and textphone **01279 663 725**

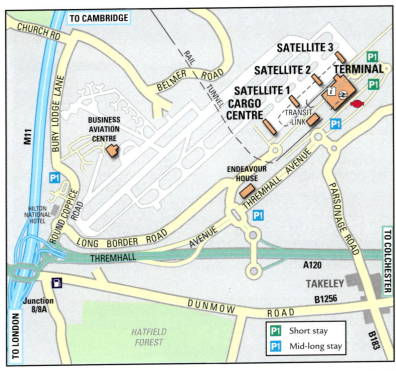

For more information, visit **www.baa.com** (look out special needs section by airport)

Help points

Free assistance is available to check-in for those with special needs. Help points are located on terminal forecourts, in short stay car parks and in the bus/coach station.

YOU GET A GREAT DEAL FROM STANNAH.

For outstanding quality and value for money you can't beat a Stannah Stairlift.

- Straight, curved or narrow staircases
- New and reconditioned
- Nationwide local branches for 24-hour backup, 365 days a year
- Emergency installations
- Full guarantee and free first service

FREEPHONE
0800 715 167 EXT 8794
stannahstairlifts.co.uk

Stannah

The world's best-selling stairlift

Bath Lift

NEW

No Batteries

No Electric

No Power to connect

The easy way to Relax & Recline in the Bath

ABLETECH Bath Lift

Send for a brochure today

Name......................................

Address..................................

....

....

....

Tel: ....

Send to:

ABLETECH BATH LIFT
Paraid House, Weston Lane
Birmingham B11 3RS
www.abletech-bathlift.co.uk

Free eye test in your own home

The Outside Clinic is a specialist in home eye care and the longest established, national, domiciliary, eye care provider in the UK

"When should I have my eyes tested?"

- When ever you have eye problems.
- Once a year, if aged over 70.
- Every 2 years, if aged 60 or under.
- More frequently, if advised by an optometrist or doctor.

"I need an eye test - but not yet"

If your eye test is not yet due but would like us to see you when it is, then register with The Outside Clinic now, and we will call you in good time to arrange an appointment.

"Who cares for carers?"

Many carers have as much difficulty in accessing opticians' services as the people they care for. If you are a carer, please do not hesitate to call the Outside Clinic if you need an eye test. We will be more than pleased to attend to your needs.

Years in practice have enabled the creation of an eye-care service that is tailor made to the "at-home" patient. The Outside Clinic is available for all those who have difficulty, regardless of age, in accessing a High Street optician. This includes, for example: those who need the assistance of friends or relatives to get out and about, or have difficulty using public transport, or have responsibilities preventing them leaving their home.

Our Service

On request, The Outside Clinic will organise your eye care in the comfort of your own home.
The sight test will involve tests to detect glaucoma, cataracts and other potential visual problems. Helpful advice and assistance is available to choose the best frames and lenses when required. The spectacles are then manufactured in a dedicated laboratory.

Aftercare

A second appointment is arranged for the spectacles to be delivered; the optical dispenser will ensure the best possible fitting for you.
As a patient you are never without optical care! Should you need any further assistance relating to your eyes or spectacles, you need only to Free Phone The Outside Clinic aftercare service. A date for your next sight test will also be recorded; as soon as it is due you will be called to make the necessary arrangements.
All patients are attended to permanently, by professionals.

FREE eye test

Eye tests are free to all patients with The Outside Clinic. There is only a visiting fee of £20 to those who do not qualify for free, NHS optical services, but even this is not charged to those who purchase spectacles.

There is no obligation to purchase spectacles. But for those who need spectacles there is a free range available to those who are in receipt of appropriate benefits. In addition, there is a choice of other frames from an extensive collection from as little as £10. For those paying privately, spectacles complete with single-vision lenses are available from £49.95 - all covered by a customer satisfaction guarantee.

Your spectacles are delivered direct to your door; you never need to leave the comfort of your own home - Nothing could be easier or more convenient.

Free Phone 0500 295 245

The Outside Clinic

The National Specialist in Domiciliary Eye Care

www.outsideclinic.com info@outsideclinic.com

Useful Contact Numbers

Department of Transport
Further information on Blue Badge Scheme policy and using the Blue Badge in Europe
Email: blue.badge@dft.gsi.gov.uk
www.dft.gov.uk

Disability Rights Commission
Independent body who enforce DDA
Tel: 0845 762 2633
Textphone: 08457 622 644
Email: enquiry@drc-gb.org
www.drc-gb.org

Travel by Bus/Taxi/Tube

Dial-a-Ride
Multi occupancy transport service, nominal charge per journey
Tel: 020 722 1234
www.tfl.gov.uk

Docklands Light Railway
Travel Hotline: 020 7918 4000

Freedom Passes
Free travel on public transport
Tel: 020 7747 4858
www.freedompass.org

London Underground
24 hour London travel information
Tel: 020 7222 1234
Textphone: 020 7918 3015
www.thetube.com

Taxicard Scheme
Travel in licensed London taxis at a reduced rate
Tel: 020 7484 2929
www.taxicard.org.uk

Car Related Issues

BBC London Travel Information 94.9FM
Updates every 15/30minutes
If you spot travel incidents:
Text: 07786 200 949

Driver and Vehicle Licensing Agency (DVLA)
Road tax exemption for disabled people
Tel: 0870 240 0010
Textphone: 01792 792 792
Email: drivers.dvla@gtnet.gov.uk
www.dvla.gov.uk

Parking and Traffic Appeals Service
Tel: 020 7747 4700
www.parkingandtrafficappeals.gov.uk

TRACE
Towed Away? Clamped? 24 hour helpline
Tel: 020 7747 4747

Other Travel Related Organisations

Mavis (Mobility Advice and Vehicle Information Service)
Practical advice on driving, vehicle adaptation and suitable vehicle types
Tel: 01344 661 000
Email: mavis@dft.gsi.gov.uk
www.dft.gov.uk/access/mavis

Motability
Wide range of cars available cheaply and easily through lease or hire purchase
Tel: 0800 093 1000
Textphone: 01279 632 273
www.motability.co.uk

Queen Elizabeth's Foundation Mobility Centre
Helpline and tuition for disabled people who wish to learn to drive
Tel: 020 8770 1151
Email: info@mobility-qe.org
www.qefd.org.uk/mobilitycentre

Tripscope
Practical information on travelling in the UK and abroad
Tel: 0845 758 5641 (local call rate)
www.tripscope.org.uk

To be included in our useful contacts section email us at **includeus@thepieguide.com**

Computer Cab plc

Suppliers of the London Taxicard scheme, with over 3,500 accessible taxis. We offer advice and support and a smooth taxi service throughout the London area.

For more information call us on
020 7908 0435

For Cash bookings call
020 7908 0207

For Credit Card bookings call
020 7432 1432

or visit www.computercab.co.uk

ComCab

If you have one of these then you should be a member of

Isn't it time **YOU** Joined **THE** organisation run by disabled people that is successful where it matters?

- Fighting for exemption from congestion charges
- Demanding better parking provision
- Lobbying for worthwhile changes to the Blue Badge Scheme
- Free information and advice service for members
- Bi-Monthly "Magic Carpet" magazine, *FREE* to members
- Discounts on Ferries and Eurotunnel
- Working for disabled drivers <u>and</u> passengers

The Disabled Drivers' Association

Freepost ANG4568 Ashwellthorpe, Norwich. NR16 1DZ
Tel: 0870 770 333   Email: DDAHQ@aol.com   www.DDA.org.uk

CHEAPEST INSURANCE?

THE CHEAPEST QUOTE
FROM OVER 450 POLICIES
ALL FROM ONE CALL
OR IMMEDIATELY ONLINE

08700 667 666

www.quotelinedirect.co.uk/quote

Quoteline Direct® part of The Wilsons Insurance Group Est 1969 Members of the General Insurance Standards Council

Directory of Services

Bathroom Equipment

Aquaneed Ltd
Lifestyle designs, competitive quotes
and professional installations
Tel: 01784 410 413
www.aquaneed.co.uk

C&B Systems
Suppliers of grab rails and sanitaryware
Tel: 020 8614 1428
www.c-bsystems.co.uk

Chapter One Group Ltd
Walk-in baths and showers
Tel: 0800 783 1912

Polypipe Bathroom & Kitchen
Products Ltd
Toilet seats for the physically impaired
Tel: 01709 770 990
www.celmac.co.uk

Abletech
Low cost, simple to use bathlift
Tel: 0121 706 6744
www.abletech-bathlift.co.uk

Sculpta Ceramics
Refresh wash basin for wheelchair users
Tel: 01782 317 486
www.sculpta.co.uk

Waterbury Bathroom Accessories Ltd
High quality chrome disabled rails
Tel: 0121 333 6062
www.waterbury.co.uk

Personal Hygiene

Arelle
Pads, briefs and accessories
Tel: 0800 389 3597
www.arelle.com

C&B Systems
Suppliers of grab rails and sanitaryware
Tel: 020 8614 1428
www.c-bsystems.co.uk

Insurance

Churchill Insurance
Churchill car insurance
Tel: 0800 032 4828
www.churchill.com

Lexham Insurance Consultants Ltd
Specialist scooter, moped, motorcycle
insurance
Tel: 0845 600 1664
www.lexhaminsurance.co.uk

Pulse
Life and travel insurance
Tel: 01305 848 850
www.pulse-insurance.co.uk

Quoteline Direct
Competitive insurance premiums for all
Tel: 0870 444 0870
www.quotelinedirect.co.uk

Vehicle Conversion

AutoChair Ltd
People, wheelchairs, scooters
into vehicles
Tel: 0800 214 045
www.autochair.co.uk

Davis Accessible Transport
Wheelchair accessible vehicles
Tel: 01732 455 174
www.accessible-transport.co.uk

Gowrings Mobility
For wheelchair and mobility access
Tel: 0845 608 8020
www.gowringsmobility.co.uk

Reselco Ltd.
Vehicles, conversions, controls,
insurance, advice
Tel: 020 8569 6363
www.reselco.com

To be listed email us at **includeme@thepieguide.com**

Directory of Services

Wheelchairs

Team Hybrid
Hand and powered cycle wheelchair attachments
Tel: 01329 830 117
www.teamhybrid.co.uk

Dan Everard Partnership
Indoor/outdoor programmable elevating powerchairs
Tel: 01223 844 280
www.dragonmobility.com

Independence Technology
IGLIDE and IBOT mobility systems
Tel: 0800 288 988
www.independencenow.com

Professional Services

MLC Disability Services
Occupational therapy services
Tel: 020 8903 4664
www.mlcdisability.com

National Centre for Independent Living
Information about direct and independent living
Tel: 020 7587 1177
www.ncil.org.uk

The Outside Clinic
Visiting opticians
Tel: 0500 295 245
www.outsideclinic.com

Consumer Research

Ricability
Independent consumer research for the disabled
Tel: 020 7427 2460
www.ricability.org.uk

Automotive Supplier

Bristol Street Motors - Bromley (Ford)
Motability accredited sales and service
Tel: 020 8249 9000
www.bristolstreet.co.uk/bromley

MAGIC
Wide range of motability and motoring info
Tel: 0800 240 241
www.fordmagic.co.uk

Vauxhall Motors Ltd
Dedicated helpline for disabled customers
Tel: 0800 731 5267
www.vauxhall.co.uk/mobility

Mobility Equipment

TGA Electric Leisure
Comprehensive range of mobility products
Tel: 01787 882 244
www.tga-electric.com

The London Mobility Warehouse
Beds, bathing, scooters, wheelchairs, lifts
Tel: 0800 093 8610
www.mobilitywarehouse.com

Sunrise Medical
Suppliers of home and healthcare products
Tel: 01384 446 622
www.sunrisemedical.com

Exhibitions

Mobility Roadshow Ltd
A showcase for new and innovative mobility products
Tel: 0870 770 3222
www.justmobility.co.uk/roadshow

To be listed email us at **includeme@thepieguide.com**

Directory of Services

Home Equipment

Advanced Door Controls Ltd
Electric door operator for single leaf doors
Tel: 01273 693 393
www.advanceddoorcontrols.co.uk

Airtec Seating Ltd
Healthcare equipment for everyday use
Tel: 0870 242 2453
www.airtec-seating.co.uk

Ascendit Lifts Ltd
Installation of domestic lifts
Tel: 01293 785 185
www.ascenditlifts.co.uk

Bakare Beds
Quality beds, quality service, guaranteed
Tel: 01752 512 222
www.bakare.co.uk

Drinkmaster Ltd
Hot drinks at your elbow
Tel: 01579 342 082
www.drinkmaster.co.uk

PCD Maltron Ltd
Special computer keyboards overcome disability
Tel: 020 8398 3265
www.maltron.com

RehabEquip Ltd
Disabled electric beds, chairs and hoists
Tel: 01483 273 587
www.4dp.com

Associations

The Blue Badge Network
Blue Badge information and advice
Tel: 01384 257 001
www.bluebadgenetwork.org

The Disabled Drivers' Association
Advice and campaigning for personal mobility
Tel: 0870 770 3333
www.dda.org.uk

Holidays

Blagdon Farm Country Holidays
5 star accessible country cottages
Tel: 01409 211 509
www.blagdon-farm.co.uk

Langthwaite Farm
Quality holiday cottages. Very disabled friendly
01524 62388
www.langthwaitefarmcottages.co.uk

Porterfield
Wheelchair accessible villa rental - Cyprus
Tel: 01702 341 178
www.porterfieldproperty.com

Educational Courses

College of North East London
Learners are at the heart of what we do
Tel: 020 8442 3055
www.conel.ac.uk

MNCS Training
Training for the carer
Tel: 01634 714 444
www.mncstraining.co.uk

To be listed email us at **includeme@thepieguide.com**

Have your say

If you have any general comments about this guide or about parking in London, the ALG would like to hear from you. You can contact them by emailing **parking@alg.gov.uk,** by phoning **020 7747 4777** or by writing to ALG TEC (Parking), 1st floor New Zealand House, 80 Haymarket, London SW1Y 4TZ.

Help required

We would appreciate your feedback on this PIE Guide, in particular classifications of car parks and petrol stations. If there are specific areas not covered by this map which you would like to see added, please let us know.

Changes

We have worked hard to compile comprehensive and accurate information in this map but we know how quickly things can change. If you find any changes, please let us know.

Online Map

As things change we will update the data on our online map until an updated map is published. You can access the online map at **www.parkingforbluebadges.com** If you would like to include this map on your website or simply link your site to it please call us on **0870 444 5434** or email **online@thePIEguide.com** to arrange this. We are happy to supply an icon for your site.

Purchase Maps

To purchase this and other PIE guides, maps or other unusual and useful items visit our website at **www.thePIEguide.com**, call us on **0870 444 5434** or email us at **sales@thePIEguide.com**.

Resellers and Distributors

To resell this and other PIE Guides please contact PIE directly on **0870 444 5434** or email **sales@thePIEguide.com.**

About Us

PIE produces customised map-based products for different community groups, including motorbike and scooter riders and mums and toddlers. Our publications also include guides to coach parking, quality ladies toilets, coffee shops and WIFI hotspots, the White Van Guide to cafes and much more. If you require a customised map, please let us know.

Would you like to see this mapping solution rolled out across the UK? To nominate a part of the UK that would particularly benefit from a PIE Guide, please get in touch, and let us know where and why. Equally, if you are interested in supporting or sponsoring our national PIE Guide, please get in touch.

Email us on **feedback@thepieguide.com** or call us directly on **0870 444 5434**